KSHIRE
CRIBED

PART OF

BUCKINGHAM SHIRE

PART OF
MID:
DLE
SEX

ART OF

Ewelme

yington-
Wallingford
ranneshe
Newneham
Bungwell
Ipsden
OXFORD
Henley

uth Stoke
deote Goring
Whitchurch
Mapledorcham
Caversham
Purley
Suthum
Tilehurst
SONNINGE
Loddon'Bridge
READING
Redding
Bradfeld
Inglefilde
Thele
Burfelde
CHARL
TONShinfelde
Vston DRED
Padworth
Stretfeld
Alder mertton
Mortimere
PART
OF WILT
SHIR
HUNDR
Silchester

Gremeland
Horspenden
WARGROVE
Shiplake
Remenham
Hurley
Bysham
BERNERSH
HUNDRED
Wargrave
Lawrence
Waltham
Ruscombe
Hurst
Billingsbere
HUND
Winkfeld
Binfeld
Warfeld
COOKHAM
Part of
Rip HUNDR
Okingham
Eaſthamſted
more Hut
Barkham
Swallofelde
Finchamſted HUNDRED
Sandherſt
Yateley
Ufkelde
Turges
Eurſley
Blackwater

Little Merlow
Great Merlow
Mr.sham
Hedsore
Thames flud
BRAYE
Topley
Madenhead
HUND
Braye
Dorney
Eaton
Vpton
Datchet
Withiahham
Chaworth
Shatsbrok
RIPPLESMORE
Windſor
Oldwinſor
Waſſbury
Winſor foreſt
HUN
Winſor park
Egham
Thameſis flud
PART
OF
Bagſhot
Sunnynghill
Colbrok

Stanes

Whitley park
Arberfelde
Part of WILT
SHIR

NORTH
EAST
WEST
SOUTH

F HAM SHIRE
SURREY

BARRACUDA GUIDE TO COUNTY HISTORY

VOLUME IV ROYAL BERKSHIRE

Newbury Cloth Hall, now the Museum.

The Barracuda Guide to
County History series

VOLUME IV

ROYAL BERKSHIRE

by
TOM MIDDLETON

Series Editor: Clive Birch

Barracuda Books Limited
Buckingham, England

MCMLXXIX

PUBLISHED BY BARRACUDA BOOKS LIMITED
BUCKINGHAM, ENGLAND

AND PRINTED BY
MALCOLM G. READ LIMITED
175 BERMONDSEY STREET
LONDON SE1

BOUND BY
DORSTEL PRESS LIMITED
HARLOW, ENGLAND

JACKET PRINTED BY
WHITE CRESCENT PRESS LIMITED
LUTON, ENGLAND

LITHOGRAPHY BY
SOUTH MIDLANDS LITHOPLATES LIMITED
LUTON, ENGLAND

TYPE SET IN TIMES ROMAN BY
MALCOLM G. READ LIMITED

ISBN 0 86023 045 7

CONTENTS

ENDPAPERS: Front - John Speed's 1610 map.

Back - John Cary's 1823 map.

SERIES INTRODUCTION

In a sense this series was conceived over thirty years ago – the product of a lifetime's work by the historian who first put it to me in 1974. Like so many good book ideas, it had failed to find the publisher who would share its author's enthusiasm. That author was the late Tom Bushell, of Chislehurst, whose *Kent* was the first volume in this series. Now another Kentish author, Tom Middleton, who hails from Tunbridge Wells and has spent most of his working life in Berkshire, has researched and written this fourth volume.

Tom Middleton already has one history book to his credit – his *Book of Maidenhead* – and as a journalist is ideally qualified to research and write about the past. His eye for detail and his instinct for some of the less obvious people and places long gone sharpens his perception and illuminates the reader's insight. The author understands the reader's needs, and knows how to communicate basic information without overstatement or dull detail. His sense of history combines with his flair with words to distill the essence of Berkshire in this comprehensive and extensively substantiated work.

The series itself is designed to give simple, easy-reference guidance to the principal people, places and events of each county's past, with comprehensive cross-reference to secondary sources for further, expanded reading and study. It is as invaluable for the generally interested reader as for the serious student, whether at school, college or simply working on a specialist study. Tom Middleton's book offers the reader a rapid but ample general record, with relevant comment unencumbered by superfluous detail.

Further volumes are in preparation, and these include David H. Kennett's *Bedfordshire* and Robin Bush's *Somerset*. It is intended ultimately to cover every county in the United Kingdom.

FOREWORD

by The Hon Gordon Palmer, OBE, TD, JP, DL,
Lord Lieutenant of Berkshire.

Before writing this foreword I picked up my copy of *Chambers'*
Encyclopaedia – which happened to be dated 1879 – and under
'Berkshire' I read such comments as:

'Berkshire is one of the most beautiful of the English
counties.'

'The Thames skirts the whole north border of the county,
winding through a course of 100 miles but in a direct line
only 72 and navigable nearly all the way.'

'The British and Roman remains are numerous, including
Roman roads and many camps and barrows.'

'Of the old castles, the principal relic is Windsor.'

I suspect that many of us who have lived all our lives in this county
know far too little about it, but now, thanks to Tom Middleton, we and
those people who speed through Berkshire by road or rail, on the way to
the West Country, will have the opportunity of being far better informed.

All those who read this book should be grateful to him for his tireless
research and for the trouble he has taken to give us, in his own inimitable
style, an enlightening and fascinating book on this Royal County of which
many of us are so proud.

INTRODUCTION

Everything has a beginning and a continuity. Thames Valley man, or to be exact, Thames Valley Woman (Swanscombe c250,000 BC) is our earliest known inhabitant. The geological clock started millions of years before that to create man's environment and what lies underfoot. It was the making of the landscape which provided the conditions for habitation and predetermined where man would go. It provided the Thames, one of man's first highways, and the Ridgeway, a first road. Human settlement began with the Neolithic people from Europe who made the first fields and habitations in permanent form. Everything that we have done has been built on this beginning. The ages of man have brought us from the first flint tool to atomic power, both local industries in their day, the one growing from the other.

Written records began in the monasteries. Archaeologists have since sifted through Berkshire sands and gravels to prehistory, recording their findings. From the Domesday Survey to modern newspapers, historians, court, council and merchant guild clerks have been meticulously recording; the divisions and sub-divisions of land are in their legal wrappings with family records, wills, inventories, plans and maps, and from the first royal charters setting up early towns and privileges to the parcels of property now being negotiated in 1979, they embrace practically every movement in the county. These scriveners and calligraphers have indexed the past.

This guide to the Royal County is an attempt to set down the historical progression of the people of Berkshire, and note how they moved on and what causes and effects influenced them. It is also an attempt to show that Berkshire began as a geographical entity and that, although smudged in outline by artificial local government boundaries and over-populated in some fringe areas, Berkshire is still a whole county, because the ancient geography of the place makes it so and influences it still.

I have relied heavily upon the help of the County Library Service and the County Record Office, without whose kind assistance this would have been an impossible task. Michael Asser, county librarian, Pat Thomas, reference librarian at Maidenhead, Daphne Phillips, reference librarian at Reading, Angela Green, county archivist, and Newbury Museum have all been extremely helpful. This is a journalist's interpretation of Berkshire's journey through the ages.

ROYAL COUNTY OF BERKSHIRE

Several explanations are given for the origin of the county's name, which undoubtedly derived from its woods and downs. Camden said it was named BERCHERIA by Latin writers. Saxons called it BEROC-CYRE. Asser Menevensis, King Alfred's biographer, believed that Barroc derived from 'a certain wood where grew plenty of box'. Early spellings included BERROCHES(S)CIRE (Domesday Book, 1086) and BERROCSIRE (King John charter, 1199).

Barroc is also interpreted as a Celtic word meaning 'hilly'; another theory is that Barroc meant Berkshire Downs, yet another that the Wood of Barroc was between Enborne and Hungerford. Another source claims that the name derived from the extensive stands of birch woods ('for which the soil was more adapted than for the growing of any other woods'). This must lead to the most poetic explanation: silver Bark-shire. It appears as Berkshire about 1300.

An Anglo-Saxon dictionary translates Baroc as 'bare oak, supposedly a reference to a polled oak in Windsor Forest where public meetings were held'. The title 'Royal Berkshire' was first used in the 1880s. The ancient, or geographical county consisted of 462,208 acres, the widest point being from Old Windsor to County Cross, Hungerford (28 miles) and the narrowest seven miles. *(22-25)*

1

Early Arrivals

Berkshire is where the Kingdom of England began. King Alfred of Wantage and the Wessex kings ensured that, bringing the whole land into one realm. But Alfred's birth is practically modern history. It took place little more than 1,000 years ago. When the Megalith Builders, who completed Stonehenge, came along the Ridgeway, it was one of only three long-distance routes in England; Julius Caesar's invasion was 4,000 years away.

Early arrivals of man in Berkshire are believed to have been about 200,000 BC. Our farming began when the New Stone Age people arrived from Northern Europe. Relics which they left behind have been found, and are still being dug up, all over Berkshire. The great monuments of Stonehenge and Avebury were built by these Neolithic people. But parts of Weyland's Smithy on the Ridgeway are 1,000 years older. Also on the Ridgeway were the county's first cultivated fields. The Neolithic people who made them were the first people to plant seed and tame animals, and the first to need storage vessels for seed and crops. From this need sprang the pottery industry.

They were followed by people of the Hallstatt culture, who came from France about 500 BC, and who developed the use of iron tools, which brought a new technology to the fields and enabled farmers to move down into the fertile valleys. Then, in the last century BC, the powerful Atrebates tribe took over Berkshire and established its headquarters at Silchester. It was there that the Romans had one of their largest cultural centres in England.

All the early invaders from Europe came up the Thames. It was the historic highway of war and trade and led to the Ridgeway and the Downs. It was also a 100 mile long defence moat for Berkshire, behind which the afforested Wessex sheltered from invasion by Northern tribes. It was from this sanctuary that the Wessex kings knitted Berkshire together, it was why Wallingford, where the Conqueror crossed the Thames, was one of the most important towns in England, why Dorchester became a place where Christianity began and why Faringdon and Wantage were established towns before many of today's great cities were ever heard of.

CHRONOLOGICAL HISTORY

70,000,000BC. Thames broke through the chalk of the Corallian Ridge to form the beautiful Goring Gap and to flow into the London Basin in the early Tertiary Period (70m BC). This determined the pattern of English life through history, providing the route for early invasions and trade. The Jurassic Seas of 100,000,000 years earlier were the probable origin of this geological phenomenon. The waters of these eruptions brought the clay that became the soil of the Thames Valley and underlaid it with the minerals we were to use for building. The limestone hills of the North Berkshire Ridge round Faringdon and Cumnor were created by the corals (hence Corallian Ridge) that grew in these early seas. It took 2,500 years to form an inch of chalk; Berkshire chalk was about 25 million years in the making.

The Thames gave Berkshire about 200 miles of river and a river highway which led to the Ridgeway. The Ridgeway (22 yards wide at the time of the Enclosure Acts) was one of three long-distance routes for pre-historic man: the Jurassic Zone from Yorkshire to the Cotswolds, the Harroway or Hardway from Kent to Stonehenge and beyond and the Icknield Way, with its continuation the Ridgeway, from the Wash to the Marlborough Downs. *(1,3,5,18,19)*

As tools improved, man moved from these first roads and the Thames to cultivate the valleys and build. The Thames Valley was one of the first places in England to be inhabited by man; earliest dated find Swanscombe Woman 250,000BC, but man is believed to have existed here in the late Pleistocene Age (1,000,000BC). *(2,3,4,293)*

200,000BC. Implements of this date found at Reading, Grovelands and Caversham, examples in Reading Museum. Largest flint hand axe in Britain and probably Europe (10,000BC) found at Maidenhead near Stone Age axe factory (see 1919). *(2,10,58,118)*

10-8,000 BC. Rhinoceros, mammoth (elephant), horse, musk ox fairly common in Europe. Skull of musk ox, first evidence that it existed in England, found at Taplow (1855), also remains of mammoth (elephas primigenius), horse (equus caballus), rhinocerosus (tichorhinus). Older pits of Taplow selected as 'type locality' for the famous Taplow Gravel Terrace, part of the flint gravel fields of the Thames Valley created by the Jurassic Seas.

Stone Age man spread all over the Thames Valley. His tools have been found at 50 sites in the Reading/Caversham area. Hundreds of hand axes of all sizes have been found from Abingdon in the north to Newbury in the South: at Wallingford, Wasing, Englefield and in the valley between Theale and Pangbourne (now occupied by the R.Pang but originally old course of the Kennet). Substantial finds were made at Maidenhead and at

Cookham Rise. At Cannon Court Farm, Maidenhead, more hand axes were found than at any other site in the Middle and Upper Thames. It is considered one of the richest palaeolithic sites in Britain. *(2,57,58)*

7,000 BC. Mesolithic (Middle Stone Age) flint factory at Newbury between present sewage outfall works and river (discovered 1920). *(91)*

3,000 BC. Neolithic (New Stone Age) finds at Braywick, Maidenhead (1975), but famous Neolithic camp, Windmill Hill, gave rise to term 'Windmill Hill culture'. Earliest Neolithic field systems (they were first people to plant seed, farm and tame animals – probably the most remarkable age of man to date) on East Hendred Down and Knollend Down, West Ilsley. Known prehistoric habitation (proof rare on Downs) at Knighton Hill above Compton Beauchamp. *(1,4,10)*

2,000 BC. Neolithic Long Barrow near Uffington, Woden's Barrow half mile south of Ridgeway, Neolithic finds in Thames south of Wallingford and Lambourne Seven Barrows, which produced one of the finest collections in the country of relics from Neolithic times, the Beaker Folk, and the Wessex cultures of the later Bronze Age. During this period the chalk lands of Wessex were the country's largest centre of population. The Icknield/Ridgeway was the only road and flint axes and cleavers were traded all along it probably from as far away as Grimes Graves, Norfolk flint mines. The Ridgeway, consolidated by the tramping feet of men and animals (no early roads were preconceived), became the High Street of history for Stone Age man. There the legends began of Magician Merlin, tutor to King Arthur, of Sir George's slaying the Dragon on Dragon's Hill and the oldest in all English History: the legend of Weyland's Smithy. It gets a mention in Sir Walter Scott's *Kenilworth*. The smithy, known as Weyland's Cave, is a Neolithic long barrow.

About this date, a potter was working at Totterdown Inkpen. The tallest beaker ever found (now in Newbury Museum) was discovered there. Potters worked there until David Buckeridge gave up at the beginning of the 20th century. The labourers who gathered the clay were known as Inkpen Yellowlegs.

Along the Ridgeway went the Megalith Builders, a jubilant people with great chieftains. They had come from Asia Minor with ideas and treasures and were the final builders of Stonehenge. At the zenith of prehistoric trade they were supreme, having trade links with Egypt.

They dealt in Irish gold, Irish axes, ornamental dress pins from central Europe, ceremonial Jadeite maces from Brittany and brought ideas from as far away as Mycenae. They built with sarsen stones such as are found at Weyland's Cave and at Ashdown House, Ashbury, where the stones are said to be a flock of sheep that Merlin petrified. *(4,27-30,34)*

Along the Ridgeway also went the Moulsford Torque: a gold necklace weighing 1 lb. It was unearthed by a ploughman on Mouldford Down (1960), the finest antique ever found in Berkshire. *(4)*

1,500 BC. Old Way, a Neolithic track, ran from Dover to Newbury and from Seven Barrows to Walbury Hill. *(91)*

1,000 BC. Bronze Age Walbury Camp at Inkpen Beacon, highest chalk hill in England (975ft). By late Bronze Age, pottery established at West Ilsley and 7,350 acres in cultivation adjacent to Ridgeway. *(4,16)*

1,000-500 BC. Large number of hill forts, probably also used for protecting flocks etc from warrior bands of La Tene culture. Area inhabited by peaceful Hallstatt culture people. *(4)*

500 BC. Among principal Iron Age sites in Britain: Blewburton Hill, Boxford Common, Knighton Hill, Long Wittenham, Rams Hill, Uffington (only one attributed to Middle Bronze Age in England). Theale and Wokingham. Also Perborough Castle near Compton, Streatley Warren (early Iron Age and Belgic finds), Wittenham Clumps, Grimsdale Castle and Dyke's Hill, Dorchester (early Iron Age and Romano-British route from Dorchester to Newbury). *4,16)*

The unique White Horse of the Vale 'a masterpiece of art'. One theory is that it dates from about the time of Christ (Berks people have not forgiven the government for moving it into Oxfordshire under re-organisation of boundaries).It is 360ft long. White Horse is a Berks county symbol. Theories of its origin include: tribal symbol of the Dobunni, who held a salient into the Vale when Berks was occupied by the Atrebates tribe based at Calleva Atrebatum (Silchester). Atrebates had bronze horse of similar design. Also said to be typical of La Tene art from Marne region of France. These people settled in Berks in Early Iron Age. *(4,7,8,9,16, 20,21,146,156)*

500 BC. Ancient ways began to change. *(293)*

400 BC. Celts came up Thames with iron swords. *(293)*

100 BC. Powerful Belgic race invaded. Tribes taking part included Bibroci (East Berks). They moved into forest. Built fort at Maidenhead (Robin Hood's Arbour). *(58,293)*

Early British coinage struck by Atrebates. *(157)*

75 BC. Belgic tribes began using heavy plough drawn by oxen. New crops: barley, millet, oats, rye. Some export to continent.

Later, under Romans and Saxons, cultivation moved downhill to richer soils. *(89, 448)*

55 BC. Julius Caesar's invasion (not a conquest, left early part of 5th cent.)

AD 2 Whispers of Christianity round Berks. *(126)*

AD 3 Reading probably dates from Romano-British of this period. Roman implements, brooches, horseshoes found all over town. First inhabitants lived on gravel terraces from Suttons Seed grounds to Orts Road and from Forbury to Lower Tilehurst. Saxon graveyards near Dreadnought Reach. Pagan burial urns in Reading Museum. Kings Road graveyard possible Christian. *(126)*

8. Saxon settlement at Old Windsor. Part of village of Kingsbury. Later Edward Confessor and Norman kings held court there. *(189)*

43. Roman station at Speen. Berks part of *Britannia Superior,* later in district of *Britannia Prima.* Conquest of Britain by Claudius. Rome ruled for next 300 years. Took over Belgic fort at Maidenhead. *(91)*

96. Until this year Atrebates retained separate identity under tribal princes. *(157)*

276. Romans (Emperor Probus) introduced vines to Britain. The Vyne (National Trust) near Silchester - The House of Wine - has bust of him.

320. Roman road system well established from Silchester. Two main roads, one from Gloucester, met at Speen. The other, via Shaw, Hermitage, Sandy Lane, Beedon Common, Stanmore, Farnborough, linked Speen with Ridgeway. *(89)*

383. Magnus Maximums declared emperor of Britain. He travelled to Silchester using the 'Imperial Post', obtaining fresh 'post' horses along the route. This is the origin of the use of the word 'post', later to become 'mail'. He called at homestead on the Devil's Highway, Finchampstead (Saxon name for old Roman road). *(295,298)*

450. Saxon invasion began. They set up seven kingdoms, among them Wessex, and defences along the Thames against King of Mercia. *(293)*

600. First wooden Wallingford Bridge built. Most historic Thames crossing point above London. Because of this Wantage became a principal township long before Oxford. Eventually Wallingford and London Bridge had 19 arches, were 900 and 915ft long. Believed designed by same man. *(157)*

636. St Birinus, after conversion of Kent to Christianity (597) by St Augustine, came to pagan Wessex on special mission from Rome. Baptised Cynegils, king of Wessex, in Thames at Dorchester where he established his See. The diocese included Hants, Wilts, Berks, Dorset and Somerset. Plaque records his preaching on Downs near Blewbury. He carried out baptisms also at Bapsey Pond, Taplow. Pond still exists. Berks remained in See of Dorchester until 705. Then: 705 to 909 See of Winchester; 909 to 1058 Ramsbury (referred to as Sonning, where bishops had palace: there was no cathedral church); 1078 to 1217 Old Sarum; 1217 to 1836 Salisbury; 1836 Oxford. *(32,189,297)*

675. Abingdon Abbey founded by Cissa, a West Saxon thane. Built of wood. Childrey gets name from stream rising in village belonging to Cilla, sister of first abbot; originally Cillarithe. *(35,36,104)*

699. King Ina founded monastery at Bradfield. *(289)*

758. Offa The Terrible, King of Mercia, conquered Kinewulf, King of West Saxons, and seized county from Wallingford to Ashbury, between Inknield Way and Thames. *(289)*

785. Offa gave Goosey Manor to the Abbot of Abingdon in exchange for Andersey Island near Abbey Gateway. Abbot's geese fattened on Goose Green. *(43)*

802. Egbert expanded Wessex, but eventually West Saxons forced back to Faringdon/Wantage area. *(293)*

832. Danes appeared round coast, entered Berks along Thames. Eventually made Reading their stronghold. *(293)*

834. Date of Parish of St James The Less. Pangbourne (rebuilt 1868). *(291)*

849. Alfred, 4th son of Ethelwulf, King of Wessex, born at Wantage Palace. Became king in 871 and reigned for 30 years. Tutored by Asser at Wantage. Further education in Rome. Adopted by Pope Leo IV as godson. Warrior, author, lawgiver, founded English Navy. Palace site probably at Belmont. His first capital of Wessex - a moveable place - was Faringdon. 'Palace' believed to have been on site of Salvation Inn. *(293,297,418)*

870. First mention of Reading in Anglo-Saxon Chronicle. Danes sacked town. *(101,108,114,126)*

871. Danes raided Reading. Fortified by Saxons. From Reading a Danish army moved to Englefield ('the field of the Anglo-Saxons') where they were defeated by Athewolf. Ethelred and Alfred his brother attacked Reading, but Danish defence held. This year there were nine battles against the Danes in Wessex, including historic Battle of Ashdown (site believed to be 25m west of Reading on Downs) where Ethelred and Alfred defeated Danes, killing their king Bacfeg. In the fighting, nine Danish earls fell. Wessex under Alfred, alone of West European kingdoms, inflicted heavy losses on the Danes. They made peace with him and withdrew to London. This was the beginning of the kingdom of England. *(126,289,291,418)*

894. Danes 'traversed Herlei [Hurley] in their march up the Tamese'. *(77)*

924. Edward the Elder, son of Alfred, died at Faringdon. He was born at Wantage. *(292)*

Abingdon Abbey refounded about this date by King Alfred's grandson, King Eadred. Ethelwold, a monk from Glastonbury (later canonised), restored abbey. He led revival of monasticism in England. Abingdon at confluence of Thames and Ock rivers. (Ock derives from pre-Saxon EHOC, meaning salmon.) *(104)*

925. Wessex's King Athelstan, Alfred's grandson, began to tidy up trading practices. His Grately Decrees allowed, for first time, small business deals outside towns. He also created first single currency for the kingdom by regulating the minting of coins. The decrees put a ceiling on the number of moneyers and stipulated where mints should be set up. This was probably an efficient re-organisation of an established practice. There was already government control over minting, with severe penalties for moneyers who disregarded it, such as having a hand cut off. *(418)*

955. First mention of parish of Compton Beauchamp in charts of King Eadred.

956. Edgar made King of Mercia. Following year, dominated all England. Styled himself *Rex Anglorum* and *Basileus.* Coins struck in this reign at Wallingford Mint (believed to have been in Goldsmith's Lane). Mint, in existence 925, continued until 1270. Moneyers received dies from Exchequer and worked subject to examinatories. They, assayists and exchequer controlled weight etc. Anciently, a mint was privilege granted to a town. *(157)*

King Edwig granted wood from Hawkridge, Bucklebury, for rebuilding church at Abingdon. *(291)*

Edwy The Fair gave 15 hides (approx 1,200 acres) to Alfwin, at Milton. Chapel built (first rector 1325). Today dedicated to St Balise, patron saint of wool-combers. Eventually, route to great sheep fair at Ilsley ran through village. Milton House has links with Admiral Benbow (see 1689). *(291)*

970. King Edgar granted land at Chilton to Abbey of Westminster. Edward the Confessor recorded two manors held by Wenric: Place Farm and Manor Farm. Both names still exist. *(291)*

978c. Mint operating at Reading. *(126)*

994. Aethelweard, first translator of the Anglo-Saxon Chronicle, buried at Mortimer. His father Kypping was lord of the manor. *(291)*

The Middle Ages

Mediaeval Berkshire was a time of many beginnings, but its principal importance to the county's social history was in the struggle between the townspeople and the monopolistic powers of the church, through the great abbeys of Reading and Abingdon. Conquest had brought extraordinary privations to England. William put his own nominees into most of the manors. The hated Odo of Bayeux, one of the leaders of the rape of England, got Taplow. Starvation gripped the land. Men fought with each other for food. It was the beginning of an age of poverty for the underprivileged that lasted for centuries.

Berkshire's economic asset was its wool. Downland sheep turned Hendred and other places into thriving communities. Newbury, Reading and Abingdon were among the most famous cloth towns in England. Their merchants were consulted by the monarch. These men, substantial burghers, and the craftsmen they employed in the cloth industry formed the merchant guilds which embraced all the trades through their ramifications. They won from the crown charters of privileges, which were how free towns began. Wallingford got its charter 30 years before the City of London. The guildhalls became the town halls of Berkshire and, eventually, the guild masters its mayors. Town fairs and markets followed in the wake of the charters, supervised by guild officers, a sort of crude consumer protection service. The power of the abbeys was broken, though not without revolt, bloodshed and burning. The Peasants' Revolt of 1381 was fostered in the anti-clerical feeling of the time.

King John signed the historic Magna Carta in Berkshire, giving man the right to be judged by his peers. Thus Berkshire remained in the mainstream of English History.

It was in the Middle Ages also that bridges began to be thrown across the Thames, that the Great Western Road was straightened to run through Maidenhead, probably for military reasons. War was an ever-present thing. In this also, Berkshire excelled. Berkshire butts supplied the cream of the archers at Agincourt.

1006. Danes pillaged parts of Berks. Reading burned and convent of nuns destroyed; Wallingford sacked by Svein Forkbeard and castle destroyed. *(101,126,289)*

1042. Household servants of Edward the Confessor (born in neighbouring Islip, Oxon) occupied 15 acres in borough of Wallingford. Edward made it a royal borough. *(157)*

1066. Six days after Battle of Hastings, Conqueror's army marched to cross Thames at Wallingford. Wigold of Wallingford, Saxon lord, supported William, who believed Harold a usurper, and allowed troops to cross. With Wantage and Faringdon, Wallingford became one of the most important towns of Wessex, before Oxford was heard of. William stayed some time. There received submission of Stigand, Archbishop of Canterbury, who had opposed him in Kent. Wigold's daughter Aldith married Norman knight Robert de Oyley (later D'Oyley) who rebuilt Wallingford Castle (begun 1067 finished 1071). Robert D'Oyley's only daughter married Miles Crispin, big Domesday landowner. *(17,292, 293)*

One of William's first acts was to recover the manor of Old Windsor for the Crown. In January, Edward the Confessor had granted the manor to the monastery of St Peter, Westminster. William began to establish a ring of fortresses round London, of which Windsor Castle was one – only one intact today. He began castle building in England. Soon crown lands were to spread round Windsor and Maidenhead. *(157,170,171,189)*

1069. William imposed curfew *(Couvre Feu)* to prevent rebellious meetings. All lights and fires extinguished by 8pm. But because of his welcome at Wallingford, their curfew was postponed to 9pm. A time of great privations. *(157)*

1079. First mention of Newbury as a separate place. Church of Speen given to the Priory of Aufay, Normandy, with local tithes. *(89)*

1084. Conqueror spent Easter at Abingdon Abbey. (His younger son, Henry I, was educated there). *(168)*

1086. Reading and Wallingford (the more important) only two fortified towns in Berks. Manor of Reading held by King. The Abbot of Battle (Sussex) also held lands given him by Conqueror as act of thanksgiving after 1066 victory. (Battle Hospital, Battle School, Battle Farm probably built on abbey lands.) Six mills built on Kennet. One, Abbey Mill, turned by Holy Brook, which with Kennet was abbey's main drain. Drinking water for abbey came from Whitley through lead pipes. *(126)*

Henry de Ferrers (see 1138), one of William's commissioners, rode into Berks to begin Domesday survey. Berks was divided into 22 hundreds; 250 entries manors or holdings, but in fact only about 200 manors; 31 churches mentioned, 65 mills, 43 fisheries. Hundred of Thatcham had 16 manors, 5 churches, 14 mills; these included a water mill at Wantage where Clark's mill stands today. One of four major nunneries in the country was at Coleshill.

Hurley Priory founded (see 1903) by Geoffrey de Mandeville. Cell of Benedictine Abbey, Westminster, at Lady Place. Pulled down (1873). Old Bell Hotel (dates from 1137) believed to be priory guest house. Hurley occupied since Bronze Age. Domesday also refers to 'ten traders before the gates of the [Abbey] Church, Abingdon. This was how the commercial town began. Berks population between 40-45,000. Desolation by conquest and pestilence carried off one third of people, but Berks third wealthiest county in England. *(38,77,78,89,289,291)*

1093. Finchampstead Church rebuilt. Village well flowed with blood at times of national disaster (local legend). *(257,296)*

1100. Faritius, doctor from Arezzo, Italy, became Abbot of Abingdon. Carried out large building programme and reformed administrative system. Obtained from Henry I right for a market at Abingdon. *(35,36,38)*

1107. Henry I took his easter court to Old Windsor's royal residence. Castle not yet equipped for such functions. *(189)*

1110. Henry I's court held for first time at Windsor. *(189)*

1121. 18 JUNE Henry I laid the foundation stone of his new abbey (completed 1124). Eight black-robed monks from Cluny in Burgundy, followers of St Benedict, arrived in Reading. Foundation charter signed at Rouen (1125). Charter stated Reading, Chelsea and Leominster had been closed because of their sins and he would refound Reading and give it the possessions of the other two. Henry I buried there in front of the High Altar. Built on site of burned nunnery (see 1006). First abbot Hugh de Boves (1123), formerly Prior of Lewis. The great monastery accommodated many kings on their visits to Reading. After Reformation was royal palace for short time. Monastic orders in Britain date from about 912. *(104,126,289)*

1125. Empress Matilda, widow of Henry IV of Germany and daughter of Henry I of England, brought to England the hand of St James the Apostle. It was given to Reading Abbey, enshrined in a golden reliquary studded with jewels. In an inventory of the Abbey in Henry VIII's time is this entry: 'Imprimis twoo pieces of the Holy Cross. Item Saynt James Hande'. *(126,231)*

1130. St Mary's Church, Cholsey, built on old Saxon foundation. Henry I gave church to abbots of Reading, who had summer residence at Cholsey, but it was older settlement. Ethelred the Unready founded it (908). Parish Registers date from 1539. Following year Alyce Wyllmott baptised. Willmott family still in village. Village Green called The Forty, believed derived from the 40 paces of archery. *(291,293)*

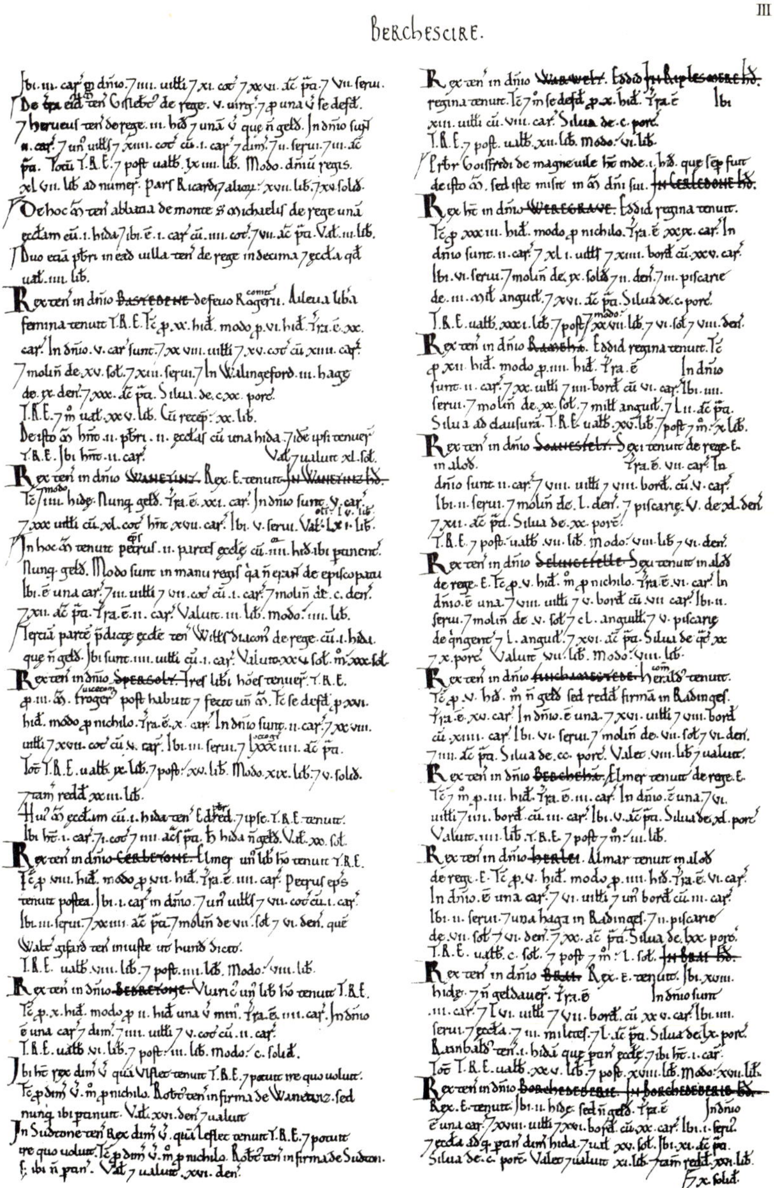

Berkshire in 1087 - the Domesday entry.

Carta regis henrici fundatoris nri de fundatione & libtatibz Eccłie Radingensis.

HENRICVS dei grana Rex Angloꝝ & dux Normannoꝝ. Archiepis. epis.
Albanbz. comitibz. Baronibz.q; suis. & omnibz xpianis tam prefentibz; qͫ
futuris: salutem ꝑpetuam. Saant quia tres Abbatie in regno Anglie ꝑ
catif exigentibz; olim deftructe sint: Radingia scilicet atq; Chealsea & Leominstia.
q̅s manuf laica diu possedit: earumq; terras & possessiones alienando diraprit.
Ego aū consilio pontificū ꝛ alioꝝ fidelium meoꝝ pro salute anime mee & Will
regis patris mei. & Will regis fratris mei. ꝛ Will filii mei. ꝛ matildis regine
matris mee. ꝛ matildis regine uxoris mee. ꝛ omnium antecessoꝝ ꝛ successoꝝ
meoꝝ: edificaui nouū apud Radingiam monastium in honore ꝛ nomine dei ge
nitrif semꝑ uirginis marie. ꝛ Beati Johannis ewangliste. Et donaui eidem
monasterio ipsam Radingiam. Chealseam quoq; ꝛ Leominstiā. cum appendiciis
suis. cum siluif ꝛ agrif ꝛ pastuns. cum pratif ꝛ aquis. cum molendinif & piscariis.
cum Eccłif quoq; ꝛ capellis ꝛ cimiteriis. ꝛ oblationibz ꝛ decimis. cum moneta et
uno monetario apud Radingiā. Dedi etiam pfato monastio thacheham. ꝛ eccł'am
de Wargraua. Ita ut quom ea in manu mea fuere: sic libera sint ꝛ absoluta & ple
na: in manu abbatis ꝛ monachoꝝ radingie. Nulla autem ꝑsona parua uł mag
na p debitū seu p consuetudine. aut p uolentiam: aliquid ab hominibz ꝛ ter
ris ꝛ possessione Radingensis monasterii exigat. ñ equitationem siue expeditioñ.
ñ pontium uł castroꝝ edificationē. ñ uehicula. non summagia. ñ uectigalia. ñ

FIG. XVI. Foundation Charter of Reading Abbey.

ABOVE: Reading Abbey's Foundation Charter, 1125.

BELOW: The Abbey gateway.

x

1135. Henry I died in France. Body sewn in bull's hide taken to Reading Abbey and entombed before high altar. Abbey now one of greatest in kingdom, its abbot among the foremost men of the realm. Abbey relics at this time said to include: a piece of Our Lord's shoe, part of Moses' rod, part of St Philip's skull, one of St Luke's teeth, the left hand of St James (see 1121, 1164, 1786). *(126)*

1138. Robert de Ferrers, son of Henry de Ferrers (see 1086), created earl. His father had acquired the Manor of Bisham. Robert gave manor to Knights Templar, the warrior monks, dedicated to protecting pilgrims. Based originally on Solomon's Temple in Jerusalem. Master sat in Parliament as chief ecclesiastical baron. Temple Mills, Bisham, dates from this period. *(78)*

1140. Robert of Gloucester built castle at Faringdon, which Stephen razed to ground. *(292)*

1142. Matilda (Stephen's Queen) fled from Oxford across frozen Thames to Wallingford Castle, her stronghold in civil war with Stephen, camouflaged in white cloak. Ensured that the old Saxon blood line of Wessex kings returned to English throne in her son, Henry II. Wallingford held out against all Stephen's efforts to subdue it. *(157,293)*

1152-3. Newbury Castle at the Wharf captured by Stephen after seige of two months with spearmen, archers and light horse. John Marshall defended it. His son William became Earl of Pembroke, the Great Protector (see 1219). *(91)*

1153. Reading Castle given up by Stephen to Henry II. It was then demolished. Old county gaol in Castle Street built on site. Traces of original structure found (1798). *(101,108,126,289)*
Appropriately, it was the Treaty of Wallingford which made Stephen king and Henry of Anjou his heir. *(157,161)*

1154. Henry II succeeded Stephen. Held first Great Council at Wallingford Castle. *(157,162)*

1155. Wallingford's Charter of Liberties by Henry II. Thirty years before City of London. Many unique privileges never before given, presumably because of town's support for Matilda. King held Great Council at Wallingford. *(157,162)*

1163. Great concourse of people and nobles on the island below Caversham Bridge to watch a trial by combat. Henry of Essex, the King's standard bearer, accused of cowardice and treachery. He denied it. King ordered trial by combat. Essex fell and the monks carried his body through the River Gate. Believed dead, he recovered and became a monk. *(124)*

1164. Henry II present at dedication of Reading Abbey Church by Archbishop Thomas Beckett. About 200 Benedictine monks, a mint and mint master. Henry spent Whitsun (1175) there, Easter (1177) and was present (1184) when Baldwin was elected Archbishop of Canterbury. Abbey grew to about size of Westminster. Mediaeval chronicler wrote of 'the unwearied and delightful hospitality of the monks of Reading'. It was full of stained glass, richly embroidered accessories and pure gold ornaments. *(104,126,289)*

1185. Heraclius, Patriarch of Jerusalem, and Roger, Master General of the Knights of the Order of St John of Jerusalem (Order survives in St John Ambulance Brigade), went to Reading Abbey to persuade Henry II to go to the relief of the Holy Lands. He refused. His son Richard, however, went and is said to have seized from the Abbey the priceless casket bearing St James's hand, when he ran out of money. *(126)*

1189. First mention of the burgesses of Newbury (in the Pipe Roll). *(91)*

1190. A charter (1139) from Bishop of Salisbury had prohibited anyone from school teaching without the abbot's consent. Another charter this year granted to Reading Abbey the School of Reading. Thus Reading School dates at the latest from that charter and is one of the oldest schools in the country (see 1625, 1781, 1871). *(108,114,126)*

Appleton Manor House dates from about this time. It is one of the oldest continually inhabited houses in England. *(291)*

1191. Richard I held Parliament in Reading Abbey. It met there again in 1213, 1341, 1263, 1440, 1451, 1452. *(289)*

1193c. Priory of St John the Baptist founded at Sandleford for Augustinian Canons. Edward II stayed there (1320). It closed in 1740, estates granted to St George's Chapel, Windsor. St. Gabriel's School incorporates some of the monastic walls. *(91)*

1199. Newbury site given to Knights Hospitallers of St John of Jerusalem, who had preceptory at Greenham. *(89)*

About this time began the disafforestation of Windsor Forest, which stretched to Hungerford. *(89)*

1204. Manor of Faringdon given to Cistercian Abbey of Beaulieu, Hants, by King John. Cistercians were great farmers. Cell formed at Great Coxwell and Great Barn built: 'finest of the surviving mediaeval barns in England and one of the most impressive structures of its kind in Europe'. Proof of huge grain production in area where Faringdon had grain market (see 1674). *(292,420)*

King John took Newbury into his own hands. Believed to have founded St Bartholomew 'almshouses'. Litten Chapel attached to old Grammar School, now commercial school (see 1466). *(91)*

1205. Thames frozen. 'On 1 January began a frost which continued until 20 March so that no ground could be tilled and frozen ale and wine were sold by weight.'

1215. Wallingford Castle, one of the most important in England because of its strategic position at the Thames Crossing, strengthened against the rising barons on the order of King John. John was frequently in Wallingford. Richard I had given him the Honour of Wallingford. *(162)*

1215. Magna Carta signed at Runnymede. Barons camped on 100 acre meadow. King John rode over daily from Windsor Castle. Barons and bishops had met at Reading and assembled on Loddon Bridge to march to Runnymede. Magna Carta Island claimed as actual site of signing (presented to National Trust by Lady Fairhaven and sons 1930) (see 1974). *(189,297)*

1219. William Marshall, the Great Protector (see 1152-3), died at Caversham.He rescued England from foreign yoke. Secured throne for King Henry. Name derived from Marshall of the King's Horse. William Marshall, 2nd Earl of Pembroke, became lord of the Manor of Newbury. *(89)*

1222. Chapelries of Sonning 'farmed out', the holders paying a fixed rent to the Dean of Sarum. There was a sort of trade in fees. Vicar of Sonning paid 40s to the Dean. Mr Hamo, who held the parishes of Wokingham and Sandhurst, paid him 2lbs of wax and sent one mark (about 7s 6d) to the Dean. But the annual chaplain of Wokingham and Sandhurst paid 10 marks to Hamo for Wokingham and one mark for Sandhurst. He in turn received 2 marks from John, annual chaplain of Sandhurst. The chaplain of Hurst, who had no land or house, had to pay 10 marks to the Dean. At this time an income of £10-20 was a competent estate for a gentleman. A sheep cost about a shilling and an ox between 10s and 12s. *(219)*

1229. Thomas Ace of Wallingford paid twopence for right to allow his pig to scavenge for food in the town's streets. *(162)*

1232. St Mary Magdalene Hospital, Newbury, dedicated to leprous women. *(91)*

1233. The Friars-minors, or Greyfriars (Franciscans), settled at west end of Friar Street, Reading. Part of friary survives. *(114,126)*
Wallingford had: 24 shoemakers, 7 bolters (millers), 17 glovers, 30 mercers (cloth merchants), 3 metal workers, 11 smiths, 13 carpenters, 7 weavers, 3 fullers (cloth workers), 16 bakers, 5 fishermen, 47 women, 63 'foreigners', 11 from Crowmarsh, 6 foreign women and 56 others. The 'foreigners' came from as far afield at Berkhamstead and Basildon. Other trades included: goldsmiths, vintners, brewers (nearly all women), fishmongers, inn-keepers, locksmiths, cutlers, farmers, dyers, shearers, corn merchants and maltsters. There were two mills. *(162)*

1234. Saint Edmund of Abingdon – he was born there – became Archbishop of Canterbury. Became greatest lecturer Oxford ever had and its first doctor of divinity. Played decisive part in preventing war between king and barons. Strong supporter of English party. A founder of Oxford University's greatness. *(38,49, 50)*

1239. Wooden bridge over Thames at Caversham replaced ford. In chapel by bridge was what one of Thomas Cromwell's agents described as 'the principal relic of idolatory within this realm . . . the spearhead that pierced the Saviour's side upon the Cross'. *(126)*
Reading cloth specified by Henry III when ordering the county sheriff to buy 52 ells (ell: 45 inches) for tunics for friars. Cloth-making a going concern from about 12th century in Reading. Nine famous clothmakers, including Thomas Cole of Reading, called by Henry I 'The Six Worthy Husbands of the West', who kept great numbers of spinners, carders, weavers, fullers, dyers, shearmen and rowers. They petitioned the king

for a measure. He measured his arm's length on a staff and said: 'This measure shall be called a yard'. Berkshire cloth acclaimed overseas. *(114)*

Black Death epidemic.

Reading monks made wine from a vineyard at Tidmarsh. *(291)*

1240. Monk at Reading Abbey wrote famous canon 'Summer is icumen in'. Earliest canon known and one of the earliest examples of English secular music. *(103)*

1242. Nobility of England converged on Wallingford, where the owner, Richard, Earl of Cornwall, and his brother Henry III gave a big Christmas party. The extremely rich Richard extended the castle and entertained lavishly there. Senchia, daughter of Beatrix Countess of Provence, was at the Christmas party. Richard married her the following year. *(162)*

Windsor Castle garrison consisted of 4 knights, 11 men, 4 cross-bowmen and seven watchmen. *(189)*

1248. Great Tournament at Newbury among the knights of England. *(89)*

1250c. Stone from Marcham quarry carted to Wallingford to build its first stone bridge on orders of Earl of Cornwall.

1250. Date of Wallingford Church. Inside is Fitzwarren brass, one of the oldest in England. *(162,168)*

1253. Reading Guild of Merchants, after long conflict with abbey, granted charter by Henry III. The guild was established years before. Its warden became first mayor. Guild mainly concerned with cloth trade, of which Reading and Newbury were centres; Reading's principal industry. The guild's cofferers acted as treasurers, constables kept the people in order and the stocks and pillory in good shape. Searchers enforced guild regulations through maintenance of accurate scales. One guild privilege was to keep swans on Thames and Kennet. Eventually there were 200. This was the beginning of local government as we know it in Reading. *(101,108,113,114,126,289,297)*

1256. Pope Alexander IV gave permission for the building of a private chapel in the thriving wool town of Hendred, now oldest part of Hendred House, where the Catholic family of Eyston has lived and worshipped since 14th century. They descend from Sir Thomas More. In house are his drinking cup, silver banded ebony staff that supported Bishop Fisher on his way to the scaffold. More and Fisher were friends. (Both canonised 1935). *(291)*

1256. Abingdon School, later Rosse's School, founded. *(35,36)*

1261. Fracas in Windsor market where the locals objected to the intrusion of Reading Merchants' Guild members setting up competitive stalls. They threw their goods in the mud and set upon them. Subsequently, Reading sued Windsor and Windsor was heavily fined. *(114)*

1267. Ochold (Ockwells Manor), set in a clearing in Windsor Forest, granted to Richard de Norreys, cook to Eleanor, Henry III's Queen. *(58,289)*

1269c. Chapel of East, around which the town of Maidenhead was to grow, set up at Maidenhead near the wide river ford. *(57,58,231)*

1272. Manor of Englefield held by Somery family. *(289,412)*

1277. Windsor's first charter made it the county town of Berkshire, because the gaol was there. But town could not afford the alms to keep the prisoners alive. Innocent and guilty died of hunger. Gaol moved to Reading. *(189)*

1280. Maidenhead ferry replaced by wooden bridge. Great Western Road diverted from Cookham to run over it, obviously for military reasons. Inn-keepers moved into High Street and highwaymen into Maidenhead Thicket. It was the beginning of Maidenhead as a communications centre. *(58)*

1284. Specialised markets running in Wallingford: corn in St Lucian's parish, linen in parish of St Mary the More, fish and meat in parish of St Mary the Less, gold in Goldsmiths' Lane. *(162)*

1290. JUNE. St Edmund's Fair began in Abingdon (see 1234) to provide funds for chapel of St Edmund. It still survives. *(38)*

1292. Manor of Erlegh St Bartholomew held by John de Erlegh, known as the White Knight. Hence renaming 'Erlegh White Knights'. Erlegh Court later owned by Sir Owen Buckingham MP, killed in duel at Stanlake, Hurst, by Richard Aldworth; later home of Henry Addington (see 1801, 1839). *(291)*

1295. Reading one of first towns commanded to send representatives to the Model Parliament. Has returned MPs without break to present day. *(126)*

1297. Treble Bell at St Lawrence's Church, East Challow, cast by Paul the Potter (1282-1312), one of the oldest signed bells in England. *(235,291)*

1300c. Bell-hanging a Berks industry. Bells cast at Wokingham hung at Chilton, North Moreton, Appleford and Didcot. Later foundries at Reading and Tilehurst. Another at Aldbourne, just over the border, moved to E. London and is now Whitechapel Foundry (see 1867). *(43,371)*

Hock Day at Hungerford originated about this time to celebrate ancient rights conferred by John of Gaunt. Held 16th day after Easter. At Hocktide, Hungerford elected a constable, portreve (town's chief officer), bailiff, tithingmen, keeper of the keys of the coffers, hayward, water bailiffs, ale-tasters and bellman. Still celebrated. Whole town takes part. Today, all the girls get kissed. *(231,395)*

1302. Thomas de Shawe and Henry de Bedford became Windsor's first members of Parliament. *(189)*

Sybil le Clerekes took sanctuary in St Michael's Church, Wallingford, after committing theft. She was allowed to leave the country from the port of Bristol. (Taking sanctuary in Wallingford churches was commonplace.) There were ample facilities: Wallingford had 11 parishes each with a parish church, and there were three other religious foundations. *(162)*

1312. Edward III born at Windsor. *(189)*

Knights Templar occupied Bisham Abbey (until 1335). Priory of Austin Canons there until Dissolution of the monasteries by Henry VIII, who founded Benedictine Abbey there which lasted only seven months. He gave estate to Ann of Cleaves, also Ives Manor, Maidenhead. Warwick the Kingmaker buried at Bisham, also young Earl of Warwick. Abbey said to be haunted by Elizabeth Hoby, who beat her son to death. Now owned by Central Council for Physical Recreation. *(58,78,291)*

John of Reading guilty of forging the king's seal. Hanged. *(126)*

1314. Edward II at Reading. His officers seized 23 quarters of oats for the king's chicken. Parliament was petitioned and payment ordered. *(289)*

1315. Effigies of Sir Robert Achard and his two wives, 'work of considerable artist', each carved from a single trunk of an oak, in Sparsholt Church. One of country's oldest churches there in 963, rebuilt 1187. Much of present building dates to 1327. Nine Men's Morris Board, mediaeval game, carved on wall. Mentioned in *A Midsummer Nights' Dream*. *(43,291,299)*

1316. Abbot of Abingdon and monks attempted river crossing in flood. All drowned. Monks built causeway (see 1416). *(293)*

1325. *Chronicon Roberti de Reding* of English History (1200-1325) written by monk of Reading Abbey. *(114)*

1326. Richard de Wallingford put an horloge (timepiece) in his monastery. Description of machine in Bodleian Library. *(161)*

1327. Abingdon only Berks town to receive summons ordering 'one or two of most discrete wool merchants of town' to attend the King at York, to treat with him concerning matters touching him on the profits of the wool merchants of the kingdom. Abingdon important cloth-making centre in 14th and 15th centuries. Declined after Civil War. Then mainly spinning and weaving of hemp and flax (see 1377). *(38)*

Armed rising against Abingdon Abbey. It controlled mediaeval life of N. Berks, monopolising trade and controlling markets and tenants, who disliked having only one customer. Out-of-town merchants excluded. Guild members, supported by Mayor of Oxford and students from Oxford University, massed for attack when the signal - a peal from St Helen's church bells - was given. First attack repulsed but large part of abbey set on fire. Next day, large reinforcements of traders moved in, and second attack was successful. The Market House, known as the Bury, burned down in the rioting. Troops eventually retook the abbey. There was a move among peasants and traders to revolt against church power, culminating in the Wat Tyler rebellion (1381). *(38,47,293)*

1337. Sir William Tressell endowed College of St John the Baptist at Shottesbrooke, one of smallest of its kind. Originally Roman occupation of parish and Roman church. These colleges took no monastic vows. Estate has come down intact from Saxon times to present day. *(58,390)*

Archers for Hundred Years' War (1337-1453) chosen from best at practice at St Mary's Butts, Reading, and other Berks archery ranges. Berkshire longbowmen were among cream of Agincourt troops. The Butts and St Mary's Church built near Olde Strete, oldest part of town. Reading sent in all 50,000 men to fight French. The armory area of town was Lormery Lane (Hosier Street) where bowyers, fletchers and lorimers (bit and spur makers) had their workshops. Edward III prohibited sport, which detracted from archery practice. *(114)*

1338. Greenham Preceptory of Knights Hospitallers. Had preceptor, brother knight, chaplain, squire, bailiff, under officers and servants. *(91)*

1345. Most Noble Order of Garter instituted by Edward III at Windsor, accompanied by pageantry, tournaments and banquets. Founder members: King, Black Prince and 24 knights. Chapel of St George, predecessor of present St George's, enlarged, re-dedicated and lavishly furnished.

6 AUG. By Letters Patent, Edward laid the foundationof his 'Colledge within the Chappell' (see 1481). *(170,171,189)*

1345. Sir Nicholas de la Beche died. He was Constable of the Tower. Monuments to family in Aldworth Church known locally as The Giants. Elizabeth I rode from Ewelme to inspect them. 'Giants' thought to be unique in England. Family castle once stood where manor house now is. *(291)*

1348-9. Black Death. Berks severely affected. Lost one-third of its people. Vicar of Sonning (Thomas de Brackeles) a victim. *(910)*
Abingdon's present 2-day Michaelmas Fair began shortly after this outbreak. JPs were authorised to fix wages, which were proclaimed at the fair. Continued to be a hiring fair until present century. Small fair held a week later – still called the Runaway Fair – at which employees could change their contracts. *(35,36,38)*

1354c. Sir Robert de Hungerford died. Inscription on memorial in Hungerford Church promising 550 days pardon, on the word of 14 bishops, 'to all such who shall pray for his soul'. His nephew, Sir Thomas, was first Speaker of the House of Commons. *(289)*

1355. Riots at Oxford University led to some students making their way to Reading Greyfriars and some to Cambridge, where they formed nucleus of new university. Abbot had given Greyfriars new site and they considered setting up alternative to Oxford University there. Lay scholars eventually returned to Oxford. No more university talk was heard until the Victorians arrived. *(114)*

1359. Wedding of John of Gaunt to Blanche, daughter of Henry Plantagenet, Duke of Lancaster, at Reading Abbey. Chaucer's *Parliament of Fowls* describes the feasting. *(104,114)*

1360. Donnington Priory, a Trinitarian House, founded. *(89)*

1362. Sir Bernard Brocas became Master of Royal Buckhounds. *(189)*

1369. Windsor guildhall built. *(189)*

1376. Priory of Crouched Friars (suppressed 1538) set up in Newbury. The Priory now occupies part of the site. *(89,91)*

1377. County population not much changed since Domesday. Heads taxed, exclusive of paupers, children and clergy: 22,723. *(289)*
Edward III summoned members of Newbury Weavers' Guild to confer on state of woollen industry. *(90,93)*

1384. Richard II, his nobles and the Mayor and Aldermen of London assembled in Reading to try John Northampton, an ex-mayor of London, for sedition. The sentence: perpetual imprisonment. *(289)*

1385. Joan, Fair Maid of Kent, wife of Black Prince, died at her principal residence, Wallingford Castle. *(157)*

1386. Donnington Castle rebuilt by Sir Richard Abberbury. Great Gatehouse one of England's finest examples of military architecture. Castle originally 150ft long and 95 feet wide. *(91,263)*

1387. Battle of Radcot Bridge. Robert de Vere, Richard II's favourite, defeated. He fled to Louvain. *(291)*

1389. Great councils and parliaments met at Reading Abbey at least a dozen times. Richard II dismissed his ministers and began personal rule. (He was murdered 11 years later.) *126)*

1399. Thomas Chaucer, son of poet Geoffrey, became Constable of Wallingford Castle. Katherine of Valois, Henry V's queen, was living at the castle with her son (Henry VI) and his Welsh guardian, Owen Tudor. *(162)*

1400. Fraternity of the Holy Cross, Abingdon, began commercial and benevolent schemes for the town, including a bridge over the Thames (see 1416) – it was to bear upon Wallingford's position as an important river crossing and communications centre - and the Long Alley Almshouses. They also set up Market Cross (destroyed by Commonwealth Forces under Waller, 1644). *(38)*
Long Guest House of Abingdon Abbey built. With Old Prior's House (c1250) it has been beautifully restored, now among few mediaeval interiors in UK. Greatest mediaeval architecture in Abingdon at St Helen's Church. Thames Street buildings alone survive from the Great Abbey. Granary (bought by Corporation 1637) used as house of correction until 19th century, converted to cottages, condemned 1934. Nearby Checker (exchequer) Hall now theatre. Long Gallery, probably last building to be added (c15th century), acquired 1945 by Friends of Abingdon. Preservation due to skill of the late W.H. Godfrey and Pilgrim Trust. *(38,39,44,45,46)*

1416. First two of three Abingdon bridges (see 1400) built by Fraternity of Holy Cross. This guild was forerunner of present Christ's Hospital. Present bridges much altered over 500 years, composite of three bridges: Abingdon over backwater, Burford (borough ford) over main stream, Hales Bridge over marsh. Thames not navigable for heavy barges between Culham and Abingdon. The Swift Ditch was used for main traffic until main arch was widened (1780). Goods unloaded at Culham went by road into town. Three flood arches added by William and Maud Hales about 1430. Monks cut present main stream of Thames. The bridge made a shorter route to Gloucester for traffic formerly using Wallingford bridge. The new structure began the decline of Wallingford. Royal inquisition later held into its decline (1438). *(35,36,38,157,162)*

1420. Reading Guild of Merchants (see 1253) found Guildhall meetings constantly interrupted by the noise outside. Building was to west of bridge joining London Street and High Street. Reading housewives did their washing in the river, beating the clothes with battledores. Guildhall rebuilt nearby. The King granted guild the abandoned hall formerly used by the Greyfriars. They had all become elderly and had been released from their vows. *(126)*

1431. Abingdon Abbey's power still resented by the free traders of the town. William Mandeville, a weaver, led second rising against the abbey (see 1327). It failed and he was executed. J.R.L. Anderson quoted *Piers Plowman* for William Langland's comment on the worldliness of the monk of his day:

'A leader of lovedays and a land buyer
A pricker on a palfrey from manor to manor
An heap of hounds at his arse as he a lord were.'

(44,46,293)

1439. Black Death depopulated Wallingford. Diversion of main road (see 1416) had taken route to Gloucester and S. Wales through Abingdon. By this year Wallingford had only four parish churches and 44 households. *(161)*

The plague of the Black Death sent Parliament to Reading. While there it instituted a new order of nobility: viscount. *(101,114,297)*

1440. Eton Collegiate Foundation with chapel begun. Later a school formed by Henry VI. Lower school contains the oldest schoolroom in Europe. Contains examples of early brickwork introduced from the continent. Eton became world's most famous public school. John Prudde, king's chief glazier, worked on college glass. North side of main quadrangle built 1440s and 1450s. Masons were recruited from Oxford and Burford. *(189,300)*

1441. Resistance to Abingdon Abbey led to formation of parish guilds. Fraternity of the Holy Cross given charter of incorporation. It maintained the bridge, met for business in the Exchequer Room in the parish church. *(293)*

1442. Ninety of Reading's principal citizens were divided into groups, each to provide one fully equipped and supplied soldier for the king. *(126)*

Bricks for the building of Eton College made at Langley kiln which was erected for the purpose: 66,000 bricks were delivered in May. In next nine years, 2,469,000 delivered from Slough brickfields. *(489)*

1443. Any Reading barber shaving a man after 9pm paid a fine of 300 tiles, used to replace thatched roofs which were a fire hazard. The fines were imposed by the guilds, many of which had roots in the Anglo-Saxon period (400-1042). They had developed from the Roman collegia.

Thrifty burghers built the town: barons and nobles were usually short of cash. Free towns, such as Reading and other Berks charter towns, worked for trade justice and good government. They were often at loggerheads with the abbeys and churchmen. Five Reading companies merged to form the Guild of Mergatory (see 1253). These were the merchants who, with the craft guilds, guarded the interests of the artisans, and were the first people to have a strategy for local trade and town layout. In Reading, crafts could only operate with a sort of planning permission from the guild. Shoemakers were restricted to Shoemakers' Row (between Forbury Gate and the Hallowed Brook). There were distinctions between the various trades and what they were allowed to do. The guilds were the town's bulwark against oppression by outside forces. They made the royal charters work. Eventually, guildhalls became town halls, the seats of local government (see 1662). *(126,297)*

1444. Brass commemorating William Fyndern at Childrey is the largest in Berkshire (9ft 6ins x 3ft 8ins). *(43,292,394)*

1448. Roger Landen had bell foundry at Wokingham. Foundry moved to Reading on his death (1495). Three other Reading foundries. *(325)*

1450. Lord Fitzwarren lord of the manor of Wantage. His daughter Alice married Dick Whittington. *(291)*

1451. 20 DEC. Letters patent confirmed a bequest by John Hosebond of £100 for the foundation of the Chantry of St Mary Magdalene in the Chapel of St Andrew (Maidenhead) and authorised the formation of a guild to be called: 'The Overseer, Warden, Brethren and Sisters of the Fraternity of Guild of St Andrew and St Mary Magdalene, Maydenhyth, who shall maintain Maidenhead Bridge and take tolls'. *(57,58)*

1452. Parliament adjourned from Westminster to Reading because of the Plague (see 1191). *(108,126)*

1459. The Beare, a pre-coaching inn (now Bear Hotel at 54 High Street) in Maidenhead, stood at 35 High Street (now Midland Bank). Here the encounter between the Vicar of Bray and James I was supposed to have taken place. The king lost his way when hunting in Windsor Forest and pulled into the inn. James hunted with the Royal Buckhounds. The story goes that the king was alone and had no money. The Vicar of Bray and his curate were dining there; the vicar refused to pay the king's bill, but the curate stumped up. The incident is part of local folklore, and may be no more than that. Officers were quartered at the Beare when troops were stationed in Maidenhead, before Windsor had a barracks. No. 35 later became the town's post office. *(57,58,298)*

1460. During the Wars of the Roses, which kept civil strife going until 1497 with continued eruptions Newbury supported the White Rose of York. There was an uprising at Newbury against the House of Lancaster (Red Rose). The Earl of Wiltshire, Lord Scales and Lord Hungerford were sent to punish those favouring the House of York. The guilty were hanged, drawn and quartered. Many inhabitants were executed. The three visitors, however, were short-lived: the Earl was beheaded, Scales was murdered and Hungerford lost his head after the battle of Hexham. *(89,91)*

1466. Parliament moved to Reading from Westminster, owing to the Plague (see 1452). *(126)*

Henry Wormestall founded chantry in Newbury Church, the priest 'techyng a gramer scole ther'. Appears to be the origin of Newbury Grammar School (see 1548). School continued in Litten Chapel. *(91)*

1476. Abbot John Saute of Abingdon granted 'form of indulgence' preserved in British Museum, one of the earliest examples of printing by William Caxton in England. *(91)*

1481. Edward IV incorporated college at St George's Chapel, Windsor, under the title of 'The Dean and Canons of the King's Free Chapel of St George's within his castle at Windsor'. *(171,188,191,201,209,214, 215,217,218)*

1483. Insurrection at Newbury. Buckingham's rising to bring about the deposition of Richard III. Berks men met there and proclaimed the Earl of Richmond King of England. The rising failed. *(89)*

1487. Reading Guild's authority extended to superintendence over the manufacturing of cloth. *(289)*

1489. Landlord of the Bear Inn, Maidenhead, charged with asking unlawful price for provisions. *(57,58,231)*

Sir Arthur Writhe (or Wriothesley) first Wallingford Pursuivant to Arthur, Prince of Wales. *(385)*

1497. Reading Guild of Merchants' feast. Menu included: beef, lamb, hens, chickens, sugar, wine, grease, flour, wode, oranges and powder. *(126)*

Sixteenth Century

Tudor Berkshire was fairly prosperous. Merchants were making fortunes, but the thumbscrew was still used to extract confessions. There was a wide gap between the people who were building the tudor mansions and the poor, yet in the towns early steps were taken towards the formation of a middle class by the artisans of the guilds. There was an advance in scholarship, a beginning for grammar schools, as the need for learning grew, and the first printing press was set up in Abingdon, which in the 20th century was to become a centre of the craft.

One of the most violent aspects of the age was religious persecution.

Prosperity came from the cloth industry. Newbury had 3 members on Grand Council convened by Edward III concerned with the trade. It now had a wide reputation overseas. Its raw material came from the flocks on the Berkshire Downs. John Winchcombe, alias Jack of Newbury, was one of the merchant princes. He was a big spender, a generous man and had refused honours offered him by the king, although he entertained Henry VIII during his progress through the county. John Kendrick of Reading was another. He became one of the town's principal benefactors. The cloth industry produced the magnificent mansion, Shaw House, and it was a Berkshire clothier who founded St John's College, Oxford. The other industry which began about mid-century was silk. Mulberry trees were first imported into Wokingham, whence the industry spread to flourish in Reading, Twyford and other parts of East Berks.

But it was the dissolution of the monasteries by Henry VIII which altered a way of life which had existed for centuries, and the talk of protestantism began to spread. Into this arena of religious controversy came another clothier's son, William Laud, during which he also championed the people of his native town.

Perhaps it was because of the needs of Berkshire merchants, clustered around the old Roman road, that the first regular postal route went by horseback down the Great Western road, with Maidenhead as one of the first staging posts. There were as yet no such things as mail coaches, although the first private coach in England was seen at Bisham Abbey.

1500. Reading's population approximately 4,700. Its growth during Middle Ages and Tudor period was due to the cloth trade. The greatest of the cloth manufacturers was John Kendrick. *(126)*

1503. Sir John Mason, born in Abingdon, became distinguished Tudor diplomat. *(38)*

1507. Brass to John Scoffyld, at Brightwell-cum-Sotwell, is the only effigy of a priest holding the Host. *(392)*

1510. Beautiful half-timbered Dorney Court built. Superb example of early Tudor manor house. *(202)*

1513. Sir Thomas Englefield, speaker of the House of Commons, died. Crown took Manor of Englefield.

Jack of Newbury, alias John Winchcombe, alias John Smallwood, married in Litten Chapel, Newbury. Jack was one of the most prosperous of all merchants and among the most famous. He had erected the first factory in England, 200 looms employing approximately 1,000 men, women and children. It stretched from Northbrook Street to Victoria Park. On visiting his house, his prospective father-in-law saw 'warehouses filled with woole, some with flocks, some with woad [plant yielding blue dye] and madder [plant yielding dye] and some with broad cloathing and kersies [coarse cloth] readie dyed and drest, besides a great number of others, some stretched on tenters [machines for stretching cloth, cf. tenter hooks] some hanging on poles and a great many more lying wet in other places'. He said: 'You be bominably rich'. He was right. Jack was 'of merrie disposition, well beloved of rich and poor, and never a churl of his purse'. A big spender. The wedding 'endured for ten days to the great relief of the poor'. There is a story of Robert Pert of Watling Street, who owed Jack money and whom Jack found down and out. He set him up in business again, and Pert became an alderman of London. This year James of Scotland invaded and Jack was called upon to equip six men for the war. He immediately cut out coats for 100 horsemen and

22

quickly made ready 50 men, well mounted, wearing white coats and red caps with yellow feathers and demi-lances in their hands. He personally let his 100 men (50 horse and 50 pikemen), who distinguished themselves at the Battle of Flodden. A poem was written about the exploit: *Newberrie Archers at Flodden Field. (89,224,227)*

1516. Beam in Lollington House, Cholsey, carved by John Wilmot (see 1130). Poet Laureate John Masefield eventually lived there. *(291)*

1518. Henry VIII went to Bisham Abbey to escape smallpox, measles and the Plague. Last recorded date when the court met at Wallingford. *(78)*

1518c. Henry VIII began a progress through Berkshire. John Winchcombe received him in Newbury. He selected 30 tall men from his servants, made them blue coats faced with scarlet and added swords and bucklers. He entertained the King and Catherine of Aragon at his house. Henry offered him a knighthood,which he declined. Jack died the following year and was succeeded by his son, John Winchcombe. *(89)*

1522. State visit of Emperor Charles V to Windsor, where he was received by Henry VIII. *(189)*
Nineteen people who died of 'asiatic cholera' buried at Wantage. *(163,286)*

1524. Priory of Holy Trinity, Wallingford, dissolved by Cardinal Wolsey to provide money for the foundation of his new college (Christ Church) in Oxford. *(162)*

1525c. Henry Seymour, clockmaker of Wantage, made famous 'faceless' clock in parish church of St Augustine, East Hendred. Still keeps good time and plays 'The Angels' Hymn' at three-hourly intervals. On St Thomas the Apostle's Day, flour is distributed at East Hendred to widows and widowers. *(291)*

1528. First printing press in Berks began working at Abingdon Abbey. (Act of 1583 forbade the use of printing presses except in London, Oxford and Cambridge). *(325)*

1529. Catherine of Aragon's staff stayed at Bisham Abbey. Cost: 10d a day. *(78)*
Title of 'protestant' came into general use at about this time, and English Reformation had its beginnings.

1534. Henry VIII repudiated papal authority and dissolved the monasteries. Newbury was one of the first Berkshire places where repercussions were felt. Christopher the shoemaker was burned at the stake; Julius Palmer, a young master at Reading Grammar School, former fellow of Magdalen College, Oxford, also Thomas Askew and John Gwyn, a weaver, were condemned in parish church and burned at the stake at the Sandpits, Enborne Road. They became known as the Newbury Martyrs. The Abbeys of Reading and Abingdon were doomed, also lesser houses at Bisham, Donnington and Wallingford. *(91,92,297)*

1536. Richard Layton and Edward Carne, following Henry's suppression of religious houses, arranged the takeover of church property in Berkshire. When they got to Bisham, Margaret, niece of Edward IV and Richard III, who had married Sir Richard Pole, was in residence. She opposed the surrender of the Austin Canons. The Canons did surrender, but Henry had presided over his council there and had a special regard for the place. He re-established it on a more impressive scale. It received the status of an abbey and its Abbot, William Cordrey, was given permission to wear the episcopal mitre. *(78)*

1537. For spreading a rumour that Henry VIII was dead, a Wallingford man was cast into the pillory and had his ears cut off. *(161)*

The Protector Somerset visited Newbury. His entourage contained 44 horses. *(89)*

1538. Abingdon Abbey surrendered its possessions to the Crown. Last Abbot was Thomas Rowland, who was given the manor of Cumnor. Abbey had lasted 863 years. There is still an Abbot of Abingdon in Rome. *(35,36,293)*

Abbey Gateway and other buildings bought by William Blackall after the Dissolution. The Corporation bought them from him. Room over gateway used as prison for 250 years. *(38)*

Greyfriars of Reading surrendered church. Nave later used as guildhall, later still became workhouse and prison (see 1233). *(114)*

Inmate of Donnington Hospital, Newbury (founded 1393), Thomas Barrie, accused of saying Henry VIII was dead. Punishment: to stand in market place with his ears nailed to the pillory. Afterwards they were cut off. Donnington became Hospital of Queen Elizabeth on her accession. Buildings date from that year. *(91,367)*

1539. Miles Coverdale, (1488-1569), first translator of the Bible into English, was living at Newbury. He became Bishop of Exeter (1551). Coverdale was a Yorkshireman. His first translation appeared in 1535 and his translation of the psalms is retained in the Book of Common Prayer. He edited the Great Bible (1539) which was ordered to be placed in all churches. (A Coverdale Bible was sold on 14 February 1977, for £30,000.) Thomas Cromwell, who masterminded Henry VIII's plans for dissolution, had agents checking on religious reforms. One reported from Newbury that priests were not energetic enough in carrying out the reforms and that certain Popish books had been found. *(89-91)*

Hugh Cook (Faringdon), last Abbot of Reading, upright and courageous, executed as traitor at Reading. He refused acknowledgement of the king's supremacy except in temporal matters and refused to surrender abbey. The Dissolution was really about the divine right of kings rather than the divine right of the Pope. Abbey fell and monks were expelled. Annual value at suppression £2,000. Henry III turned part of monastic buildings into a palace. Cook's trial said to have taken place in the room above the Inner Gateway which, much restored, still stands as part of the Shire Hall site. Some 228 volumes from abbey library are catalogued. Most famous and beautiful is the endless canon 'Summer is Icumen in' (see 1240). *(39,104,389)*

Facsimile score of 'Sumer is Icumen in.'

John Speed's plan of Reading, 1610.

xii

Reading Corporation resolved that one of its MPs should be a burgess. Normally they were chosen by the Corporation, but sometimes the High Steward (who offered to pay their 2s a day expenses) picked both of them. *(126)*

Bere Court, Pangbourne, county residence and chapel of Abbots of Reading, passed to Sir Francis Englefield. *(291)*

1541. Henry VIII used dissolved Reading Abbey as one of his palaces. *(289)*

1545. Ladye Place, Hurley (Convent dedicated to Virgin Mary), given to Leonard Chamberlayne. Later property of John Lovelace. His grandson, Sir Richard, went on expedition with Sir Francis Drake and is said to have built the mansion with part of the proceeds. His son, Richard, became Baron Lovelace of Hurley. *(58,289)*

1547. Thomas Teasdale born. His support for Abingdon scholars led to foundation of Pembroke College, Oxford (1624). *(35)*

1548c. Newbury Grammar School founded. *(89)*

Earliest known map of Wallingford Castle. *(162)*

1549. Images and tabernacles taken out of St Laurence's Church, Reading. The new Prayer Book in English was coming into use. *(126)*

1550. Edward VI granted Reading Abbey to Protector Somerset. Rebuilding of Parish Church of St Mary started. Dismantling of parts of abbey caused Henry I's tomb to be broken up and his bones scattered. Poor knights' lodgings at Windsor Castle rebuilt with stone from the Lady Chapel. *(104)*

1552. Edward VI visited Reading. Met by Mayor and aldermen at Coley Cross. Mayor presented him with two yoke of oxen, then rode before him bare-headed to the palace. Royal visits to abbey as a palace numerous. *(289)*

Bisham Manor granted to Philip Hoby,emissary of Henry VIII. The two brothers, Philip and Thomas, demolished the Priory Church and removed the tombs of the earls of Salisbury, including Warwick the Kingmaker. A plate originally fixed to the foundation stone of the abbey, commemorating the victory of Edward III and the 3rd Baron Montacute at Halidon Hill, later turned up at Denchworth, near Wantage. Another relic, an effigy of the father of Richard Neville,1st Earl of Salisbury, the Kingmaker, was discovered in Burghfield Church. *(78,79,85,86)*

William Dunch moved to Little Wittenham Manor. He was auditor of the Royal Mint for Henry VIII and Edward, Esquire Extraordinary to Elizabeth, Sheriff of Berks and MP for Wallingford. (One member of Dunch family staked and lost Wittenham Manor to James II in a card game.) *(43)*

1553. Thomas Dolman, clothing factor, retired to Manor of Shaw and began building Shaw House, which became a magnificent mansion. *(89,90)*

Abingdon Almshouses in St Helen's churchyard built by Master and

Governors of Christ's Hospital, a body which was founded this year. It originated in two mediaeval guilds: the Fraternity of the Holy Cross and the Guild of Our Lady. *(38,41)*

1554. Elizabeth confined at Bisham Abbey by Mary, in the care of Philip and Thomas Hoby. Alterations made to abbey for Elizabeth's comfort, including the addition of an oriel window. *(78)*

1555. Sir Thomas White, son of Reading clothier, founded St John's College, Oxford, to 'strengthen the orthodox faith'. White made a fortune as a merchant tailor, became Lord Mayor of London. Endowed scholarships at Reading School. Archbishop Laud (see 1573) was a White scholar. *(126)*

Lead taken from Wallingford Castle to make water pipes for Windsor Castle. *(161,172)*

Dorney Court, Dorney, became home of Sir William Garrad, Lord Mayor of London. A younger daughter (he and Lady Elizabeth had 15 children), Martha, married Sir James Palmer of the Sussex family of Palmers. The Palmers are still there. Present owner: Colonel P.D.S. Palmer. *(202)*

1556. Abingdon county town of Berks, with population of approx 1,500. (By 1901 it had only risen by another 5,000.)

Charter incorporating Borough of Abingdon and confirming its market. Both market and town fairs held continuously from about 1100s. Charter secured by Sir John Mason, educated at Abingdon Abbey, ambassador to France for Henry VIII, Clerk of the Privy Council, Chancellor of Oxford, Dean of Winchester. *(35-39)*

Sir Thomas Hoby of Bisham Abbey, sometime ambassador to France, owned one of the first private coaches in England. General travel by waggons and coaches was about a century away. *(232)*

1558. Philip Hoby of Bisham died at Blackfriars (May 29). Body taken by Thames to Bisham for burial (June 9). Abbey bequeathed to his half-brother Thomas (aged 28), who married Elizabeth, daughter of Sir Antony Cooke, a tutor to Edward VI. Became Sir Thomas and Lady Hoby. She was a Greek and Latin scholar. Thomas also a scholar, wrote books including *The Book of the Courtier* (a best seller), influenced creative work, became ambassador to France. Second son, born after his death, named Thomas Posthumus. Shakespeare used him as model for foolish Sir Andrew Aguecheek in *Twelfth Night. (78)*

Mulberry trees sent to Wokingham at the start of the silk industry, which was to flourish there. Silk worms that fed on them were reared in sheds heated by dung. Women said to have carried batches of eggs in their bosoms, in sewn up bags, to hatch them. Wokingham silk stockings gained national fame. Silk industry also in Reading, where its peak came in 1730, at Newbury and Kintbury, and at Twyford, where it continued until 1835. *(325)*

1559. Reading given charter by Elizabeth I which set up a common council for local government. Crown made grants for repair of bridges, including 50 oaks and 200 loads of stone from abbey ruins, gave lands and rents to meet the salary of the Master at Reading School and gave Corporation right to appoint the Master. *(101,108,126)*

1560. Edward Hoby of Bisham born. He was to translate the works of foreign scholars. Friend of William Camden, who praised Edward's scholarship in his *Britannia* and dedicated his *Hibernia* to him. *(78)* Cumnor Manor, former residence of the Abbot of Reading (when deposed), leased to Anthony Foster, steward of Sir Robert Dudley. On 8 September Dudley's wife Amy Robsart was found dead at the foot of the stairs. Did she fall or was she pushed? It is one of Berkshire's mysteries. Sir Walter Scott's account *(Kenilworth)* said to be based on Ashmole's 'unreliable account of her death'. Amy's husband was thought to have aspired to the hand of Elizabeth I. Scott made him the villain. *(292,293,347,354)*.

1563. Abingdon Grammar School re-founded by John Rosse (aged 63) for 63 free scholars (see 1256). Stert Stream flowed through school yard; believed to be the cause of several headmasters dying of the Plague. Learning, law, administration had all grown out of the abbey. John Rosse's school was in the lodgings of the hospital's officials. The sick ward became a court. Other parts of the ancient site converted to modern government in later years (see 675). *(35,48)*

1564. Much unemployment in Newbury marked a decline in the cloth trade there. This was increased by the retirement of Thomas Dolman, who bought manor of Shaw and began building magnificent mansion there. His father William had been Jack of Newbury's manager. Thomas acquired great wealth. Today Shaw House one of finest Elizabethan mansions in the country. Part of it now used as girls' school. *(89,90)*

1568. Queen Elizabeth made royal visit to Reading Abbey, now a palace. She made other visits there in 1572, 1575, 1592, 1602, 1603 and had a pew in St Laurence's Church. *(108,126)*

1569. Plaistow Green Farm, Cranbourne, built as hunting lodge. *(291)* Commissioners for muster in Berks produced lists of men able to bear arms as musketeers, archers or bowmen, pikemen and billmen. *(89)*

1571. John Rosse, founder of Abingdon Grammar School, died. *(48)*

1572. Queen Elizabeth visited Reading. St Laurence's Church accounts have this entry: 'For washing against the Queen's coming to town 4d'. *(108,126)*

1573. William Laud born in Broad Street, Reading, He was short and nicknamed 'little Vermin' and 'little hocus pocus '. His father was born at Wokingham where his mother, Lucia Webbe, lived in Rose (then Roth) Street. Her brother was Sir William Webbe, Lord Mayor of London (1597). She married first Sir John Robinson and afterwards William Laud, clothier of Broad Street, Reading. The future archbishop was educated at Reading Free Borough School. Became fellow of St John's, Oxford, its president and chancellor. Put University Press on sound basis, cut down the ale houses from 300 to 100, had High Church views. He became Bishop of Bath and Wells (1626), Privy Councillor

(1627), Bishop of London (1628), Master of the Ecclesiastical Situation (1629), Archbishop of Canterbury (1633). Ordered altars at east end of churches, introduced surplices, encouraged archery and other sports on Sundays, angered Puritans who called him a Papist. He was King's right hand man during the 'Eleven Years of Tyranny' (1629-40) when no Parliament was called. He was a benefactor of Reading, obtained its charter. Executed 10 January 1645. *(255,260)*

1574. Queen Elizabeth entertained by Sir Edward Unton at Wadley House, Faringdon. Made Henry Unton her ambassador to France. Unton descendants (including J.R.L. Anderson, author of *The Upper Thames*) still living in Faringdon area. *(293)*

1575. Thomas Dolman died (see 1564) and Shaw House completed (1581) by his son John. *(89,90)*

1578. Elizabeth confirmed setting up of the Guild of the Overseer, Warden, Brethren and Sisters of the Fraternity or Guild of St Andrew and St Mary Magdalene, Maydenhyth (Maidenhead)   (see 1451). *(57-58)*

1579. The post as we know it today began. One of the first regular routes was down the Bath Road. Maidenhead was one of the first staging posts. Elizabeth's order was for a postal service 'towards Ireland from Bristol'. Along this route went the first parcels mail. Post began with royal despatches in Persia. First post in England (15th century) the Merchant Strangers Post. Henry VIII appointed a master of the King's posts and established post houses on main roads. Royal messengers rode relays of horses. First public postal service organised (1635) by Thomas Witherings. GPO began public services 1637. Post boys carried mail until the arrival of coaching. The mail coach era lasted from 1784 (q.v.) to the arrival of the GWR in the 1840s. *(58,298)*

1581. Edmund Campion, Jesuit priest of Lyford Grange, Charney Bassett, captured after celebrating mass (later canonised). Charney Manor, once grange of the abbey, contains some of England's finest mediaeval buildings. *(291)*

1582. Maidenhead officially began. Elizabeth's charter made it a free town and its inhabitants a body corporate under the name of 'The Warden, Bridgemasters, Burgesses, and Commonalty of the town of Maideneth', a market to be held every Monday, fairs on the Feasts of St Mary Magdalen and St Andrew (patron saint of fishermen) and a court of Pie Poudre established. Corporation to consist of one warden, two bridgemasters and eight burgesses. *(57,58,68)*

1586. 'Reading's neat streets, fine buildings, riches and reputation for cloth goes beyond all other towns in the country . One order: 16,000 coats and pairs of breeches for troops. *(114)*

Chief Justice Sir John Popham given Littlecote by Wild Will Darell. Thought to have been a bribe. Local legend of a child burned to death; theme used in Sir Walter Scott's *Rokeby*. Darell said to haunt local roads at night (see 1643). Littlecote's collection of armour one of finest in

England, also includes Chief Justice Popham's chair and the thumb-stocks he used for extracting confessions. *(231)*

1589. Englefield passed to Earl of Essex. *(291,301)*

1590. The hundreds were made liable for the robberies committed within their boundaries. Hundred of Beynhurst (which included Maidenhead Thicket) paid £225 compensation for highway robberies. Vicars of Hurley, who travelled to Maidenhead once a week, drew £50 a year to cover risks of robbery on the Thicket. *(231,310)*

1592. Queen Elizabeth and court moved to Bisham. Villagers performed pageants with decorated vehicles. Privy Council met at Bisham. Queen stayed six days. *(78)*

John Kendrick (1573-1624) took over flourishing Minster St business, Reading (104 looms). He, with William Laud, had been pupil at Reading Free School. Several hundred workers at looms. Kendricks traceable to Celtic nobility. John 5th generation, became merchant prince. Company of Merchant Adventurers carried Kendrick London Cloth overseas. Reading's narrow streets filled with heavy waggons loaded with bales of wool and dye stuffs. Packhorse trains moving from clothiers through muddy streets. Dogs and hogs roaming there. Council employed 'dog whippers' to chase them out of churches. Rats numerous and carrying disease. *(225,230)*

1596. Bere Court, Pangbourne, country residence and chapel of abbots of Reading. Bought by Sir John Davies, then passed to Sir John Breedon, who built and endowed Breedon School. Trust still exists. *(291)*

1596. Newbury Charter of Incorporation. *(89,90)*

1597. Act vesting the administration of town lands at Wantage in 12 governors. Followed complaints of abuse against 'the poore town of Wantinge'. It provided income for relief of poor, mending roads and maintaining schoolmaster. Grammar school probably originated in this trust. *(163)*

1598. John and Richard Gregory killed playing football at the Moretons. *(43)*

Seventeenth Century

By the middle of the 17th century, Berkshire was torn by Civil War, the cloth industry was about to crash and even the rich were impoverished by the cost of the conflict. Charles I, who was to spend his last days in Berkshire and say his farewells to his children at Maidenhead, brought about the Civil War through autocratic behaviour at a time when breakaway religious groups were seeking more freedom and the towns were trying to acquire more independence. Thousands of troops lived off the county during the two battles of Newbury and the seiges of Reading and Donnington Castle. There was enormous destruction of property.

Shaw House became a stronghold of the King and members of the same family fought on opposite sides. Cromwell had his headquarters at Windsor.

John Kendrick's bequest to Reading, to provide work on a vast scale for the unemployed, was abused by cloth manufacturers who used the facilities to undercut competitors. There were lootings, public whippings in the market places and men were press-ganged into the army and treated like criminals. Enormous numbers of poor and homeless families were calling for work.

The Baptists and the Friends were becoming active in this atmosphere, including William Penn of Twyford, as a result of which he and a number of Berkshire people were to leave England for America to found Pennsylvania, USA.

At the beginning of the century, Sir Thomas Bodley of Holyport founded the Bodleian Library at Oxford, which was to become a powerhouse of protestantism, and at the end of the century, a revolt planned at Hurley was to bring about the Glorious Revolution of 1688 and the Declaration of Rights on the accession of William III. This stand against the House of Stuart, which altered the course of English history, was the last revolution in England, accomplished almost without the spilling of blood. It ended where it had begun, at Maidenhead, with desertions to the Prince of Orange, who was welcomed into London by its Berkshire Lord Mayor, Sir Robert Clayton.

One other revolution, which was to make Berkshire a leading county in its field, was about to begin. Jethro Tull was born here. He speeded up the progress of agriculture by bringing machines into the fields with his Horse Husbandry.

1600. Reading's population approximately 4,700. *(126)*
About this time Marc Antonio de Dominus, Archbishop of Spalato, became Dean of Windsor and rector of East Ilsley. He was 'fat, irascible, pretentious and avaricious'. First person to explain phenomenon of the rainbow. *(291)*

1601. Hungerford townsmen built, at own expense, town hall, shop, two prisons and corn market. Erasmus Webb built market house for butter, cheese and other commodities. Prison called The Blind House. *(54)*
Sir Francis Walsingham, secretary of state to Queen Elizabeth, took over Englefield House from Earl of Essex, who was executed. Ghost of Powlett Wright, a former owner, said to haunt it. Elizabeth I (and Elizabeth II) visitors. Chantry of monks once lived in its Norman church. *(301)*

1602. Flowers and rushes strewn on floor of St Laurence's Church, Reading, when Queen Elizabeth attended. She sent many mulberry trees to Reading to encourage the silk industry. *(126)*

1603. Sir Walter Raleigh brought to Maidenhead for conspiracy trial. Court probably moved out of London because of Black Death. Believed to have been held in Greyhound Inn, one of best in England. He was discharged. *(58)*

Edward Standed built manor house, Arborfield Hall. It became Aberleigh in Mary Russell Mitford's *Our Village. (291)*

King James I and Queen at Newbury. *(89)*

1605. Crown and Thistle Hotel, Abingdon, built. Name commemorates union of England and Scotland. *(38)*

1606. Englefield family bought Whiteknights, Reading, later owned by Duke of Marlborough; became centre of Roman Catholicism in area. *(114)*

1608. Monument to Sir John Croke and wife Elizabeth Unton (see 1574) and 11 children, showing what they became. Two judges (Sir John and Sir George). Sir George delivered minority judgement in John Hampden case, declaring royal attempt to levy taxes for ship money illegal. *(293)*

1609c. Sir Thomas Bodley bought Lynden Manor, Bray, which he gave to Oxford University to support public library (now Bodleian) which he founded. *(58,61,289)*

Newbury weavers established in Cheap Street, Northbrooke Street and Bartholomew Street. *(89,90)*

William Goddard died. Founded Jesus Hospital, Bray, and 40 alms-houses. (*The Harbour of Refuge* by Frederick Walker ARA, now in Tate, painted here*) (58,61,62)*

Purley Hall (originally called La Hyde) built by Francis Hyde. Later owned by Edward Hyde, Earl of Clarendon and Lord Chancellor. Hydes went into exile with Charles II in Belgium. Anne Hyde married Charles II's brother (later James II) and was mother of Queens Anne and Mary. *(291)*

1610. Famous Harwell cherries sold at Abingdon market. *(291)*

First map of Reading made. *(126)*

1611. Newbury guildhall erected. *(89,90)*

John Blagrave died. Son of John Blagrave of Bullmarsh near Sonning, 'flower of mathematicians of his age'. Nephew Daniel signed Charles I's death warrant. Left £10 a year as marriage portion for maidservant of 5 years' faithful service. Boy from Reading School drew the lots annually. Sixty poor householders received presents and escorted winner home. The charity continues. *(126,130,303)*

Also Blagrave Street, Reading.

Church of St Michael, Cumnor, contains chained Bible of this date, lifesize statue of Elizabeth I brought from gardens of Cumnor Hall, also letters from Amy Robsart to her husband. Cumnor Place former home of Amy. *(291,347,354)*

1612. Reading burghers to keep 3 leather buckets of water with which to fight thatch fires. Tax levied for hooks and ladders to prevent casualties in fires. *(114,126)*

King James came to Reading. *(114,126)*

1616. William, Lord Knolles, created Viscount Wallingford. *(289)*

1618. James Montague, Bishop of Bath and Wells, died in London. He had requested burial at Bath. Funeral procession went down Bath Road. Parishes rang bells as it passed. First night, stopped at Reading; mourners and retainers occupied two inns. Second night stop Marlborough, when followers required four inns to accommodate them. Details of funeral expenses etc in Bodleian Library.

1620. Date of Pigeon House, Eastbury. Once priory of monks of Wallingford. *(291)*
East Ilsley, centre of downland corn and sheep trade, granted charter by James I. Said to have 'sprung phoenix-like from the ashes of a town'. Once Nachededorne (from thorn tree on hill summit around which druid priesthood assembled). Alfred smashed Danes here, then Danes destroyed Nachededorne. New town Hildesley, later Market Ilsley, built round the hill of the thorn tree. Charter began its great trade (see 1750) which was seriously to injure Wallingford. *(226)*

1622. Will of Henry Fulker: 2 kine, 2 calves, one barren heifer, one bullock of a year old, £6 10s; two little mares, 30s; 5 sheep, 20s; four hens, one cock and two geese, 4s; two small pigs, 8d. His descendant Edward Fulker retired as Head Porter at Shire Hall in 1977.

1623. Francis Norreys (or Knolleys) shot himself with a cross-bow. Died without issue. Thomas Howard (1625) created Earl of Berkshire. Henry Bowles Howard 4th Earl, succeeded to earldom in Suffolk and the titles were united. *(289)*
Reading Corporation called clothiers before them for explanation of the serious unemployment in the town. The seasonal sight of streets full of loaded waggons carrying cloth to London was in decline. Among proposals for helping poor were proceedings against immigrant traders. Records name blacksmiths, doctors, tailors and teachers of dancing who were not burgesses. John Kendrick's bequest had set up workshop called the Oracle, a complex fitted with machinery and covering nearly 2 acres, to relieve the poor. Wealthy clothiers had taken it over and used the subsidised factory to undercut competitiors. Bankruptcy and unemployment followed (see 1628, 1633, 1639). *(126,297)*

1624. Two ale-tasters - Reading Corporation officials who checked for watered beer - sacked for favouritism. *(129,114,126)*
Eighteen Reading men, press-ganged into army, held in Compton prison (opposite St Laurence's Church). Greyfriars Church also used as house of correction. Inside were the old, orphans, the poor and the criminals. They spun flax and made rope. From both places prisoners were led to the market place for punishment, to be whipped or clamped in the pillory or stocks. *(126)*

1625. Charles I last king to stay at Reading Abbey Palace. London had the Plague. Law courts also at Reading, two in Great Guest Hall of Hospitium which since Middle Ages had been home of Reading School. Divided (1578) when Corporation made upper storey town hall (see 1190). With courts of star chamber, chancery, common pleas etc went 'the usual swarm of card sharpers, tricksters and thieves' in their wake.

32

Judges lodged at Bear Inn. *(101,108,126,289)*

1627. William Craven (1606-1697) knighted by Charles I, eight days later became Baron Craven of Hampstead Marshall, then member of Permanent Council of War. (Hampstead Marshall originally the home of the Earls Marshall). *(291,346,348)*

Jesus Hospital, Bray, founded by William Goddard of Fishmongers' Company. *(58,61,289)*

1628. Alms folk of Abingdon wore handmade silver badges. (On display at Christ's Hospital.) *(38)*

Hurst bowling green said to have been laid for Charles I. *(291)*

South Moreton villagers fined for failing to practise archery.
Dunch clan of N. Moreton related to Oliver Cromwell. *(291)*

Reading workhouse (the Oracle) completed. Extended from Minster Street to Gun Street astride Holy Brook (see 1633). *(230)*

1630. Rectory and parsonage of Wokingham leased to Thomas Barker of Chiswick by Dean of Sarum. Lease passed to his heirs during natural lives of William Barker, Thomas Barker and Henry Barker. Henry, then aged 22, held the manor of Buckhurst, Wokingham. *(219)*

'Great Clamour of divers poor people lackyinge work . . . in spinnyinge and cardyinge' in Reading. *(230)*

Hungry mob looted corn carts in Newbury bound for Reading. Among steps to deal with distress: 27 ale houses closed. *(91)*

1631. Sir Henry Savile of Hurst, warden of Merton College, Oxford, founder of Savilian Professorships, died. *(363)*

1633. Ludovic Bowyer had his ears nailed to Reading pillory. The letters 'L' and 'R' (liar and rogue) were branded on to his forehead. *(126,129)*

Clothiers petitioned Privy Council, which sent William Laud to investigate monopoly of cloth trade and abuse of subsidised work at the Oracle. *(230)*

1638. Plague hit Reading. Spread from house in Minster Street throughout town. 'Searchers', usually women, appointed to discover victims, who were nursed in wooden hospital on Whitley Hill. Local tax levied to pay searchers and relieve suffering families. Black rats, dogs and hogs that roamed the streets also a menace to health. Mastiffs kept by many citizens. *(126)*

William Laud obtained charter for Reading, under which the town was governed until 1835. *(225-260)*

1639. Kendrick's Oracle at Reading crashed. Looms sold (see 1623, 1628, 1633). *(230)*

Silver cups, tankards of this date, also pewter, 16th century trenchers (wooden platters giving rise to phrase 'good trenchermen') and Bowyer vase, which Lloyds Coffee House gave to Admiral Sir George Bowyer of Radley Hall for defeating French on Glorious First of June 1794, in Abingdon Corporation Collections. *(38)*

Privy Council sent Archbishop Laud to reform Reading Workhouse (see 1633). Partly successful, but Civil War intervened and workhouse became barracks. John Kendrick's will declared that if his bequest to Reading was misused the cash should go to Christ's Hospital, London. Hospital got it in 1849. *(126)*

1640. When Charles I attempted to arrest five members of the House of Commons, he was prevented by the Speaker, William Lenthall of Besselsleigh Manor. *(43)*

Reading people claimed the right to a say in the choosing of their MPs. From the election to the Long Parliament, they won the right to vote. *(108,114,126)*

Nonconformists (Baptists) became established in Reading. Its official records began 1656. *(126,331,386)*

Newbury Baptist Church founded. *(96)*

1642. Dr. Edward Pococke appointed professor of Arabic at Oxford by Archbishop Laud and made rector of Childrey. Later, tried at Wantage by Cromwell's Commissioners as 'an ignorant minister'. *(163,303)*

Petition from Berks to Long Parliament. Subject: state of the Church, with demand for measures against Roman Catholics and request for speedy consideration of clothing trade, chief support of the poor, and its general decay, 'whereof may breed great mischiefs'.

1642. Charles I left Windsor Castle for Oxford (to be his HQ). Civil War about to rage through Berks and impoverish it. Divided loyalties throughout Berks.

4 NOV. Charles (via Edgehill – first battle – and Banbury) reached Reading. The Parliamentary Governor, Henry Martin MP of Hinton Manor, had said happiness did not depend on kings; Charles ordered high treason charge. Martin fled with small garrison; had given £1,200 to Parliamentary cause and raised regiment of foot. Mother buried at Longworth. Charles commandeered tailors within 6 miles radius to clothe army, others built fortifications. Abbey Church nave blown up for stone, even wool bales used in barricades, some as high as houses.

17 NOV. Reading heavily taxed to pay for it all. Foraging parties seized food, citizens imprisoned for ransom. Defenders: 3,000 foot, 300 horse. *(262-65,291)*

1643. Essex ordered to march from Windsor (his HQ) to Oxford and take Reading. Charles garrisoned Faringdon, Abingdon, Wallingford, Newbury, Donnington, Hungerford. Roundheads moved to battle stations. Earl of Manchester's troop quartered in Maidenhead. On Maidenhead Thicket, brigade of 16,000 foot and 3,000 horse mustered. Reading Governor, Sir Arthur Aston, built forts at Forbury, Pangbourne Lane, Harrison's Barn. Reading School became powder magazine.

16 APR. Roundhead batteries opened fire with heavy guns taken from Tower of London. Reading surrendered 27 April. Essex marched away in July. Heavy casualties. *(58,261-65)*

Richard Weaver raised troop of horse in 'little forest town of Wokingham'; rode to join similar force raised by Sir Richard Harrison at Hurst. At Littlecote, Colonel Alexander Popham raised Popham's Horse. Littlecote was Roundheads' rendezvous.

34

20 SEPT. First battle of Newbury. Newbury of great strategic importance. Puritan in sentiment. Essex reached Enborne (19 September). Charles spent night in Cheap Street. Royalists drawn up on Wash Common (10,000 men); Essex had 8,000. Indecisive battle. Weaver's and Harrison's troops largely destroyed. Local street names - Essex, Charles, Battery End, Cary Close, Falkland Road - recall the famous who took part. Mounds near recreation ground mark graves of dead. Sixty cart loads of dead taken to Newbury. Charles visited wounded at Cope Hill hospital, now cottages. Retiring Roundheads surprised Prince Rupert at Padworth Gully; 300 killed. Donnington Castle (model of military architecture) held for King by Sir John Boys (previously owned by Thomas Chaucer, son of Geoffrey).*(261-65)*

1644. 27 OCT. Second Battle of Newbury. Earl of Manchester marched from Clay Hill, Rushmore Green, to attack Shaw House. Charles had dined there previous night.Thomas and John Dolman (see 1533) garrisoned this magnificent mansion. To mount front and rear attack, Roundheads marched 13 miles in 12 hours: Hermitage, Chiveley, North Heath, Winterbourne, Boxford, Wickham Heath to Speen. King took flight. Some Royalists pursued to Shinfield. Waller's Commonwealth troops destroyed Abingdon's Market Cross. Cromwell quartered at Bradfield. *(89,264)*

1645. Major-General Browne held Abingdon against heavy odds. He smoked out cavaliers from Barton Court. *(261-265)*

Cromwell failed to take Sir Robert Pye's Faringdon House. Rye's son held commission in Roundheads and was in assault on his father's house. It surrendered following year. *(261-265)*

1646. Wallingford Castle fell to Cromwell. Ordered its destruction (1653). Stone used to build St Mary's church tower. *(161)*

Berks villages lost a lot of church spires in war. Chiveley gained life-size blue boar (Blue Boar Inn), brought by Roundheads. James Hyde (Charles' executioner) came from Marcham, Thomas Trapham, who embalmed his body, from Culham. Tutts Camp, Bradfield, named after General Tutt. Charles' chaplain was rector of Bradfield. Cromwell stayed in oldest house in Curridge, Lindley Farm. Sir Henry Marten (see 1642) signed Charles' death warrant. *(291)*

Cromwell trained new Model Army (22,000) at Windsor. At one time 2,000 more troops than population there. The Blues originally Cromwellian, Lifeguards and Grenadiers Royalist in origin. Coldstreamers formed by Monk under Commonwealth. Monk, 1st Duke of Albermarle, brought about restoration of Charles II. *(189)*

Edward Pococke (see 1642) who edited missing versions of New Testament, brought cedar seed back from Aleppo. Grew present Childrey cedar, now 27ft in girth. *(43)*

Richard Aldworth founded Bluecoat School, Reading. A governor of Christ's Hospital, he decreed uniform should be similar. *(114)*

1647. Hungerford Town Council sold some of its beehives. Council produced honey and wax from 1487. *(54-56)*

Charles bade farewell to his children at old Greyhound Inn, Maidenhead. Cromwell said to have been in watching crowd. *(58)*

Elias Ashmole, who lived at Englefield, founded Ashmolean Museum, Oxford. Wrote *Antiquities of Berks*. Friend of John Tradescanth (cf. herbaceous plants, tradescanthias) who bequeathed museum to Ashmole. Ashmole, having sent last load of rarities to Oxford by barge, wrote: 'This afternoon I relapsed into gout'. *(303)*

Charles a prisoner at Caversham Castle. William Marshall, Earl of Pembroke, regent during minority of Henry III, had died at castle. *(58,291)*

1648. Thomas Kendrick, last to follow family trade of cloth-making, inherited wealth from father, William. Lived at tudor Whitley Park Manor, Reading, penniless, through war. He was a Royalist (see 1592). *(230)*

Charles spent last months at Windsor Castle. Executed 30 Jan. Embalmed body taken to Castle 7 Feb.; secretly buried next day in St George's Chapel. *(170-172)*

First town and tradesmen's tokens issued for local circulation at Wantage. 10 tradesmen or innkeepers at Wantage and one in each of following: Blewbury, Hagbourne, Harwell, Longcot and Longworth. Two issues at Steventon. Tokens had value of one farthing. *(163,305)*

1649. Cromwell visited Newbury. *(89)*

William, Earl of Craven, of Hampstead Marshall aided Charles II with money. Became devoted to Queen of Bohemia. Died unmarried (1697). Family still there (1977). *(291,303)*

1650. Reading Workhouse (the Oracle) (see 1639) full of homeless families after war. *(230)*

Hind's Head Hotel, Aldermaston, in existence. Brewed own beer until 1912. *(471)*

Wallingford mace made. Used as model for House of Commons mace (replaced two silver maces made 1615). *(157,161)*

1652. Berks Baptists' Association formed. *(331,386)*

Reading's ale houses included one in Reading Gaol. *(126)*

Private traders of Newbury issued tokens for 'necessary change'. No copper coinage issued during Commonwealth and Protectorate. *(89, 305)*

1653. Newbury burdened by 100 Dutch prisoners from Dutch War. Admirals Van Tromp ('an admiral brave and bold'), De Ruyter and De Witt met Commonwealth leaders. *(89)*

1654. John Evelyn, on Berks journey, dined at Windsor and Hungerford. Called Hungerford 'a towne famous for its troutes'. Samuel Pepys also wrote: 'so come to Hungerford where very good troutes, eels and crayfish'. *(54-56,171)*

1655. Yew tree planted at Waltham St Lawrence Church. It is still there. George Fox (founder of the Society of Friends visited Reading. William Penn (founder of Pennsylvania) also active there. *(355,399)*

Court Leet reported 30 freeholders within Borough of Newbury. *(89)*

1658. John Savage, Beadle of Hungerford, paid 2d for whipping Dorothy Miller. Public flogging of women was allowed until 1791. *(54)*
Great fire of Hagbourne. Cottages which once joined East and West Hagbourne destroyed. Londoners subscribed to relieve poverty of the village. After Great Fire of London (1666), East Hagbourne sent cash to Londoners. Blotting paper said to have been invented here by accident. Date unknown. *(291)*

1659. Walter Bigg of Wallingford gave £20 annually for a schoolmaster. He was a local man who became Master of the Merchant Taylors' Company. Pupils were taught in Town Hall attic. *(157-162)*

1660. Reading rejoiced on restoration of monarchy; king's arms added to town mace. Charles II welcomed in Windsor. Created first English standing army in following year, with 3 companies stationed at Windsor. *(101,189)*

1661. Fuller's *Worthies of England* published, relating story of turncoat vicar of Bray. Writer of well-known song altered the dates. *(58,62,289)*
The Swan, Arborfield, built. *(291)*
Reading Workhouse restored by Corporation in fight against acute poverty and unemployment. Unemployed and beggars rounded up and set to work in cloth industry revival. Experiment failed. *(230)*
Reading Abbey site granted to Sir Thomas Clarges, who sold it to John Dalby and Anthony Blagrave. *(289)*

1662. Christopher Fowler imprisoned in Windsor Castle because of religious views. Founded Congregational Church in Reading. *(333)*
Reading cobblers petitioned against shoemakers for mending and repairing contrary to regulations of the Guild Mergatory. *(114,226,297)*
Hampstead Lodge planned by Balthazar Gerbier, an imitation of Heidelberg. *(299)*

1663. Sir Thomas Dolman of Shaw House entertained Charles II and his court after their visit to Newbury. *(89)*
Henry Lucas' will bequeathed money to found Lucas Hospital, Wokingham. Drapers' Company trustees. *(219)*

1664. William Milton, Presbyterian, ring-leader of riot over election of Newbury church warden. Newbury non-conformists numbered 40. *(91)*
Newbury Company of Clothiers and Hatters formed. *(91)*
Remenham population wiped out by Plague. *(291)*

1665. Society of Friends began meetings in Maidenhead area; connections with William Penn, born Ruscombe. Town of Maidenhead, New Jersey, USA, re-named Laurenceville, believed to have been founded by Maidenhead Quakers. *(58,399)*
First pineapple in England grown at Dorney by gardener Rose and presented to Charles II. An inn at Lake End, Dorney, called the Pineapple, commemorates the event. *(202)*
Ashdown House built by Earl of Craven (see 1649) for beautiful Elizabeth of Bohemia, 'The Snow Queen', daughter of James I. Ashdown's old blacksmith's shop now factory producing road-brushing

and snow-plough products sold all over Europe. House now National Trust (see 2,000 BC). *(291)*

1666. George Villiers, 2nd Duke of Buckingham, began building Cliveden, Taplow. Architect, Captain Wynne (or Winde), associated with original Buckingham Palace, also built for Duke. Finished 1667. *(63)*

Edward Polehampton, a destitute boy, helped by landlord of Rose & Crown, Twyford. Polehampton became rich in London. Founded Twyford charity. Wee Waif Cafe there commemorates him. *(289, 291,461)*

1668. Duke of Buckingham eloped with Countess of Shrewsbury, Anna Maria. Husband 11th Earl pursued them and mortally wounded in duel, commemorated by flower bed at Cliveden and Alexander Pope's poem. Guilty pair returned to Cliveden, where Buckingham died. Cliveden bought by Lord Orkney, first Englishman to bear the rank Field Marshal; married Elizabeth Villiers. Her advice sought by statesmen of all parties, entertained crowned heads there. *(58,63,171)*

William Penn (see 1655, 1665) left for America.

Samuel Pepys stayed at the Antelope, Abingdon. Attended St Edmund's Fair. Talked to scholars, heard 'good musick, sang and danced till supper'. *(38)*

Lord Clarendon inherited Swallowfield Manor. Architect Talman (assistant to Sir Christopher Wren) enlarged and improved house and gardens. Later owned by Thomas Pitt, whose grandson William spent holidays there. *(416)*

1671. New town hall (the present one) built at Wallingford. *(162)*

1672. Maidenhead Baptists formed. Held secret meetings as dissenters. *(58,331,386,387)*

1673. Stage coaches running from Windsor to London. *(91,231-240)*

1674. Manor of Coleshill passed to wife of Thomas Pleydell (see 1768 & 1956). *(291)*

Jethro Tull born at Basildon (where he is buried) (see 1701). *(292,303, 382)*

1675. Present Braywick House built for Sir William Paule (knighted Windsor 1671). Cromwellian associations. Royalist prisoners held there. Adam Brothers added new wing for Lord Coleraine. *(64)*

1677. Post roads: Maidenhead, Reading, Newbury, Marlborough, Bristol; and Nettlebed, Gloucester. *(298)*

Mulberry tree at Old Rectory, Letcombe Bassett, planted about this time. Still alive 300 years later. Dean Swift (1667-1745) wrote under it. (Cresscombe in Thomas Hardy's *Jude the Obscure* is Arabella's Cottage near watercress beds). *(291)*

1678. Thomas Hearne of Shottesbrook born (see 1695). *(58)*

Building of Abingdon County Hall begun by Christopher Kempster, a Wren mason who helped build St Paul's. *(38,42,299)*

1679. John Evelyn visited Cliveden. *(63)*

ARTICLES

Of Agreement
Concluded and agreed on by His
EXCELLENCY

Sir Tho. Fairfax,

Generall of the Forces raised by the
Parliament on the one part:

And Colonell *THOMAS BLAGGE*
Governour of *Wallingford* on the other part:

For and concerning the rendring of the Garrison of

WALLINGFORD

Castle and Towne.

Read in both Houses of Parliament upon
Fryday 24. July 1646.

Published by Command.

London printed for *John Wright* at the
Kings Head in the old Bayley. 25 July 1646.

Conclusion to the Wallingford Siege of 1646. (JD,SD)

An enlargement of part of J. Kip's 1709
engraving of Windsor. (RS)

xiv

1680. Catherine Wiggins of Sottwell (Brightwell cum Sotwell) made oath that Mary Webb was buried in woollens only according to Act of Parliament, before Mayor of Wallingford. Act was Government effort to bolster failing wool trade. *(291)*

Unofficial house-to-house delivery of post began in Maidenhead, for which a charge was made. *(298)*

1681. Angier almshouses, Wallingford, founded. *(161)*

1682. Obadiah Blagrave, at Reading, published *An Introduction to Astrology and Epitome of the Art of Husbandry. (101)*

Lord Norris created Earl of Abingdon. *(289)*

1683. Quakers became established in Newbury. *(91,355)*

1684. Newbury prison built. *(89,90)*

1685. Newbury Corporation claimed fishing rights in Kennet. Three arrested for fishing there. *(89,90)*

John Hill of Newbury, grocer, and 10 others indicted for being absent from church. A number of Quakers were indicted. *(89)*

1686. Newbury Tailors' Company formed. *(89)*

1687. Present Windsor guildhall started (completed 1690). Original design by Sir Thomas Fitz, surveyor of the Cinque Ports. He died in 1689 and Windsor-born Sir Christopher Wren took over. *(89)*

1688. Lord Lovelace of Ladye Place, Hurley, with Earls of Devonshire, Derby, Danby, Shrewsbury, Lumley, Compton, Russell and Sidney, met at Hurley to plot overthrow of James II, a Catholic, and replace him with James' daughter Mary. This was the beginning of the 'glorious revolution of 1688'. William of Orange landed at Torbay in November and began triumphal march to London through Newbury, Farnborough, West Ilsley to Milton House, where he slept. He first met James II's messengers at the Bear, Hungerford, and stayed with Sir Thomas Dolman at Shaw House. From there he rode over to Abingdon to receive news that James had fled. Tremendous welcome in Newbury. Crowds covered roofs and filled windows, cheering his banner 'The Protestant Religion and the Liberties of England'. His army contained 'whiskered infantry of Switzerland' never before on English soil, Swedish horsemen in black armour and fur coats, companies of gentlemen and pages, the Prince on a white charger attended by 40 running footmen, Count Schomberg, first soldier in Europe – resigned the truncheon of a marshall of France for the true religion – 21 brass cannon, each drawn by 16 cart horses. Clashed with Irish Catholic garrison at Reading. Drove them to Twyford. Only officer in Prince's army to be killed lost his life here. Final battle at Maidenhead. Sir Robert Clayton of Hall Place, Burchetts Green, Lord Mayor, received Prince in London.

1689. 18 FEB. William and Mary proclaimed King and Queen of England, Ireland and France. *(58,231,306,344)*

Upper School at Eton begun. *(300)*

John Benbow ran away to sea, became famous Admiral. Pub, Admiral Benbow, commemorates his family link with Milton manor house. Peter the Great visited him there. Present Inigo Jones house built 1630. First post-Reformation Catholic chapel to be built in private house in England. Bryant Barrett, subsequent owner (1768), was lace manufacturer in Strand. Descendants still there. *(43,291)*

1690. Reading gave jubilant welcome to William III on Castle Hill. *(126)*

1692. Joseph Butler born at Wantage. Became Bishop of Bristol (1737), Bishop of Durham (1750). Wrote *The Analogy. (163)*

1694. Stage coaches licensed by Act of Parliament. *(231-240)*

1695. Thomas Hearne, son of parish clerk at White Waltham, adopted by Francis Cherry of Shottesbrooke Park, the non-juror, man of learning and piety. Hearne became antiquary at Bodleian, edited Leland's papers, which had been written for Henry VIII. *(58,303)*

1696. Earliest trust deed of Maidenhead Congregational Church. *(57,58)*

Eighteenth Century

While the cloth towns switched to brewing beer – there were 104 pubs in Reading – the county's trade was based on agriculture and the most valuable animal was still the sheep. The Ilsley sheep fair was the largest in the country, excepting only Smithfield. The problem was to move the produce of agriculture, and it was solved by the development of waterways. Rivers and canals were more important than roads to traders, and the town of Reading had the standing of an inland port at the junction of the Thames and the Kennet. With the completion of the Kennet and Avon Canal, a network of waterways linked the county with the system which included the north midlands and the North and Irish Seas.

Many roads were almost impassable and some towns practically isolated. Because of the shortage of money, the building of turnpike roads began. New roads were eventually built linking Reading with Theale, Maidenhead and Oxford as the coaching era got under way. But the route by road or river was hazardous. There were no locks on the Thames above London until Boulters was built. Cargoes were lost and men were drowned when barges capsized over weirs. At one time, all obstructions to the course of the river were illegal. Footpads and highwaymen preyed on the coaches.

With the development of agriculture and the introduction of machinery, riots began among labourers fearing loss of work. Bad wages in the industry led to the Speenhamland Act, which made the labourer dependent upon parish alms.

The Downs, which from earliest time had been the heart of Berkshire, were to be put to yet another use and become world famous for it: racing. The Duke of Cumberland, who had the finest stud in the kingdom at Windsor, began the training gallops on Lambourne Downs. Another sport, cricket, began at Maidenhead.

Politically, parliamentary candidates were having to work a little harder for their votes, for the right to vote was given to townspeople who paid scot and lot: in effect, ratepayers. Another change was the Enclosure Acts.

1700c. Alexander Pope, linen draper (father of poet), gave up business and retired to Binfield. Pope wrote *Windsor Forest* (1713). *(171)*

Reading had 104 pubs to serve population of 8,000 (by 1846 there were 21 breweries). It switched from cloth to beer. *(114)*

County population 75,000. *(289)*

Bad roads cut off some towns. Wallingford, Wantage, Faringdon suffered because there was no spare cash, but an Act of Parliament appointed trustees to set up turnpike roads. *(163)*

1701. Jethro Tull (born 1674) farmed at Howberry near Wallingford and perfected his drill for drilling peas, beans, wheat etc, which made him famous. His writings produced the new husbandry. His work translated into French (1753). Voltaire was a disciple of Tull. He moved to Prosperous Farm, Hungerford (1709), where he died 1741. Best known book his *Horse Husbandry.* He was outstanding among long line of Berks agriculturalists. His system of pulverisation allowed him to grow wheat for 13 years on same land without manuring. His experiences contained in *Horse Hoeing and Husbandry* (see 1733). *(292,303,382)*

1705. Mediaeval lamp found at St Leonard's Hill, Windsor. It is now badge of the Society of Antiquaries. *(189)*

1707. Thatcham Chapel bought for 10s by Lady Frances Winchcombe and presented to Blue Coat School, which she founded in the village. *(231)*

1709. Ranelagh School, Cranbourne, founded for 20 boys and 20 girls: known as the Green School. *(358)*

Riot at Newbury during attempt to impress a vagrant into the Queen's service. Act of Parliament said that vagrants and idle persons should be impressed. *(89)*

Bath Road accurately measured for the first time.

1711. Ascot Racecourse founded by Queen Anne. It originated at Charles II's old course on Datchet Meads, where Queen Anne used to drive her chaise. The Queen had begun to develop Windsor Park, planting Queen Anne's Drive towards Ascot (3 miles).

11 AUG. First race run. Society women attended. The riding habit now worn was seen for the first time in public. But the fashionable Miss Forrester, a maid-in-waiting who dressed like a man, according to Swift, is credited with beginning the Ascot tradition of a fashion display for women. *(307-309)*

Palmer Schools, Wokingham, founded through bequest of Charles Palmer, doctor of physic of Arborfield, and Martha Palmer of Wokingham. *(219)*

George Blagrave brought an action against the Rev William Gostwick, rector of Purley, for not keeping a bull for the use of the parish. Rector won. (Thomas Canning, brother of Prime Minister Canning, is buried at Purley.) *(291)*

1713. Mary Kendrick died aged 21. Last to bear the family name in Reading. Brought up with three sisters at the Manor House, Whitley Park. Her elder sister Frances was high-spirited, unconventional, a dashing beauty and constant source of anxiety to her mother. She left Whitley Park to live at Calcot Manor, where she became the subject of the 'Ballad of the Berkshire Lady'. Frances set her cap at a young lawyer, Benjamin Child, socially beneath her. She wanted to marry him. Anonymously, she challenged him to a duel in Calcot Woods. He was amazed that his masked opponent was a woman. The challenge was: 'Fight me or marry me'. She gave him an hour to think it over. He married her at Wargrave on 28 March 1707. Frances died 1722; Calcot Manor passed to Benjamin Child. He sold it to John Blagrave, who built existing mansion (now Golf Club). There is a tombstone erected to Alcohol in adjacent estate. Kendrick Vault at St Mary's, Reading. Benjamin died 1767. The ballad:

'It was I that did invite you,
You shall wed me or I shall fight you,
So now take your choice, said she.
Says he: Madam pray what mean ye?
In my life I ne'er have seen ye.
Pray unmask, your visage show,
Then I'll tell you aye or no.
I will not my face uncover
Till the marriage rites are over,
Therefore take you which you will: ·
Wed me, Sir, or try your skill. *(230,350,396)*

1714. Roads to Theale and Maidenhead from Reading ordered by Act of Parliament. Also, new road built: Reading to Oxford via Wallingford. *(126)*

1715. Christopher Wren, son of the architect, one of Windsor's Tory candidates. *(189)*

Act of Parliament to improve Kennet navigation to Newbury. Barges carried 50,000 tons a year of Reading's total trade. Only 100 tons went by road. *(126,278-280)*

1718. First record of Hungerford Town Hall being let for a public performance. *(54)*

Lord Cadogan, who succeeded the Duke of Marlborough as commander-in-chief, bought Caversham estate and built 'one of the noblest seats in the kingdom'. *(291)*

1720. Mob of Reading barge owners and tradesmen smashed up navigation works on River Kennet. They included the mayor and the recorder. The improvements (see 1715) made the river navigable to Newbury. Previously Reading was the distribution centre for the area. *(126,294)*

Wallingford Brewery opened by Edward Wells. Became one of largest in county; produced Wells' porter for invalids. Eventually taken over by Ushers. *(162)*

1723. *Reading Mercury,* one of the country's oldest weekly newspapers, founded. 'Mercury' was an early title for newspapers.

Kennet improved navigation (Reading to Newbury) completed. *(278-280)*

1726. Great flood demolished arch of Newbury's wooden bridge. *(89,282)*

1727. Building of Radley Hall began. Now a public school, Radley College was founded by Dr William Sewell. *(299,358)*

Stag and Hounds, Binfield, converted to an inn. William Cobbett had 'excellent breakfast' there. Outside is huge elm bole, said to have represented the centre of Windsor Forest. Binfield was one of 16 divisions known as walks in the Forest. Half-length brass memorial in church to Walter de Annefordhe is oldest in Berks. *(291)*

1728. At Aston Tirrold and Aston Upthorpe, where there is long tradition of Presbyterianism before 1662 Act of Uniformity, one of first Presbyterian chapels in county built. *(291)*

Hall Place, Burchetts Green, bought by Sir William East, who built present mansion. In Nelson's Field, trees said to have been planted in the formation taken up by Nelson's ships at Trafalgar. Highwayman Claude Duval worked the area which adjoins Maidenhead Thicket. Several reports of hauntings: Druids said to haunt the house, reports of ghostly horse and coach crossing back lawn and ghost of black servant seen at Black Horse Bridge. *(58,312)*

1730. Farley Hill Place built for John Walter. *(299)*

1731. Brimpton Mill one of the largest built in the South, for corn and later timber. Currently home of Earl and Countess Lloyd George of Dwyfor.

1733. Scandalous vicar of Beenham Vallance (1733-1752), the Rev Thomas Stackhouse, author of *History of the Bible.* Noted drunkard. Wrote most of his history at Jack's Booth, retreated to church on Sunday, breaking into incoherent prayers and maudlin tears, asking forgiveness and promising reformation of his ways. *(291)*

Horse Hoeing and Husbandry published by Jethro Tull (see 1674, 1701) *(292,303,382)*

1734c. Thomas Dicker a clock-maker and bellfounder in Reading. *(325)*

John Shute Barrington (1st Viscount) died at his seat,Beckett. Through his connection with the Harburg Lottery, was expelled from the House of Commons (1723). He assumed sub-governorship of the Harburg Company, of which the Prince of Wales was a governor, at express command of the King. Barrington thought to have been a scapegoat for royalty. *(303)*

1738. Frederick, Prince of Wales, lived at Park Place, Remenham (home of ravens).

1739. John Wesley in Reading. S. Richards built meeting house in London Street; Wesley preached there several times. Methodist Society in Reading broke up 1804, re-formed 1811. *(126)*

Frederick, Prince of Wales, rented Cliveden, Taplow (see 1666). Son of George II and father of George III. He lived there in the grand manner. He commanded first performance of Thomson's *Masque of Alfred* by Drury Lane Company; played in Rustic Theatre at Cliveden. Music included Dr Arne's *Rule Britannia!* which was first performed there. At Cliveden, Prince received fatal blow from a cricket ball. *(58,63)*

1740. John Clark sentenced to death for robbing the Duke of Marlborough's coach between Reading and Maidenhead of £90 and for commission of 23 other highway robberies. Tried at Leicester Assizes. *(234,494)*

1741. Nicholas Pocock (1741-1823) born. Descended from Pococks of Chiveley. Marine and landscape artist. In 1804, with 15 others, founded Water Colour Society, now Royal Society of Painters in Water Colour. Family lived at Ray Lodge, Maidenhead. Isaac won Royal Institution's 100 guinea prize for his *Murder of Thomas A'Beckett. (479)*

Dean Swift wrote *Free Thoughts on the Present State of Affairs* at Letcombe Bassett. He had retired there in 1714. *(289)*

1742. A Reading stage coach and a second on the Henley-Oxford run robbed on Maidenhead Thicket by two highwaymen 'well mounted who behaved with as much civility as their profession will allow of'. *(494)*

1743. Maidenhead Corporation leased to John March a strip of land on Bucks side of Maidenhead Bridge to make a way to his inn, the Orkney Arms, later Skindles Hotel (see 1833, 1914, 1918). *(58)*

Beginning of Royal Berkshire Regiment. On 25 December, Colonel Trelawney's Regiment formed in Jamaica by volunteers due home on leave. In 1748 it became the 49th Regiment of Foot. At Morpeth (1756) 66th Regiment of Foot formed. In 1782, when regiments of the line were linked to counties, these two became the 1st and 2nd battalions of the Royal Berks Regiment. The 49th fought in American Revolutionary War (1775-78), where at Brandywine Creek they dyed their hat plumes red. This was continued in red backing to their cap badge or scarlet plume-shaped flash on cap or shoulder. The 49th also sailed as marines under Lord Nelson to induce Danes to forswear their part in Act of Armed Neutrality. In commemoration, regimental bands continue to play *Rule Britannia!* after regimental march (see 1739). Royal Berks guarded Napoleon on St Helena. Designation 'Royal' granted by Queen Victoria (1885) for gallantry in the Sudan. It was the first time a regiment had received the title for gallantry in the field. *(287,288)*

1745. Bribes in Reading General Election as high as 30-40 guineas. Secret ballot ended bribery, because no check could be kept on the voting. *(126)*

1746. Boulters Lock built, the first above London Bridge. It was then attached to the Bucks bank. Boulting was a milling term. Ray Mill at

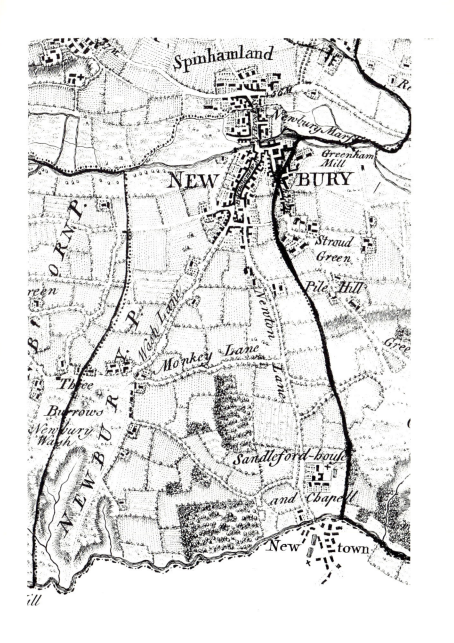

Mapmaker John Rocque's survey of Newbury, 1761.

John Treacher of Sonning's account book, 1770. (AP)

xvi

Boulters Lock was one of 28 between Oxford and Staines. Most were there at Domesday (see 1829). *(58)*

John Williams, alias Thomas Watkins, sentenced at Abingdon for highway robbery on Maidenhead Thicket. *(234,494)*

1748. Temple Mills, Bisham, making brass and copper pans, thimbles and pressing oil from rape and flax (see 1788). *(289)*

1749. Sir William Blackstone, who in 1746 was called to the bar but failed to attract either notice or practice, became Recorder of Wallingford. In 1753 he lectured at Oxford on the laws of England. Appointed first Vinerian professor; 1761 a King's Counsel; 1763 Solicitor General to the Queen. Published his *Commentaries on the Laws of England,* which earned him a fortune (see 1769). *(303)*

1750. East Ilsley corn market biggest in county, shipped grain by barge to London. Sheep market increasing in importance (see 1794). *(226)*

1750c. Mrs Montague's literary parties of the Blue Stocking Society at Greenham Priory. Name originated at these parties, attended by Benjamin Stillingfleet, who wore blue worsted stockings. Became term of disparagement for learned women. *(351,352)*

1751. Thames Commissioners set up. Control of the Thames outside London non-existent in some places, except for riparian owners, who appropriated most of the rights. The commissioners were soon heavily in debt (see 1857). *(294)*

1752. Newbury 'Flying Coach' started and Speenhamland became famous coaching centre. Flying Coach drove from White Hart to London in 12 hours, fare 10s. *(89,231-233, 240)*

1753. Smallpox outbreak in Newbury (see 1780). *(89)*

Chantry House, Bray, built. Became workhouse, infirmary and local gaol. *(61)*

1754. Anthony Addington MD left Reading for London. He had set up a home for mental patients and was known locally as the 'Mad Doctor'. He cured Chatham and his second son, William Pitt. Attended George III (1788). Spent his last years in Reading, died 1790. His son, Henry, intimate friend of Pitt, MP for Devizes (1784). Until 1795 concerned with proceedings against Warren Hastings. Lived at Woodley, formed the Woodley Cavalry, a volunteer troop under his command. Became 1st Lord of the Admiralty and Chancellor, first Viscount Sidmouth. King assigned him White Lodge, Richmond Park. *(303)*

Sarah Deacon, who had illegitimate child, sent to house of correction by Newbury magistrates for a month and ordered to be publicly whipped every Friday between 2 and 3 in the afternoon. Ann Fisher (1757) ordered to be whipped on Market Day at the public whipping post for stealing a leg of pork. *(89)*

1755. 2nd Duke of Cumberland built Fort Belvedere, Sunningdale. *(291)*

First scouring of the White Horse of Uffington followed by sports: pack sword play or cudgel play. Prize won by Tim Gibbons, local blacksmith of Lambourne, said to have left trade to become highwayman. Following year there was horse racing for a saddle, bridle and whip. Cart horses in harnesses and bells ran for a Thill harness (carters rode in smocks without saddles); flitch of bacon for an asses' race. Other prizes: waistcoat, cheese and silk hats. Cudgel playing for gold-laced hat and buckskin breeches. Wrestling for silver buckles and pumps. *(146)*

1756. Stubbings House, Maidenhead, built by C. Ambler.
Field Marshall Conway built Ragged Arches Bridge (Wargrave - Henley Road) from Reading Abbey ruins. Lombardy poplars at Park Place first to be introduced to this country from France. Field Marshall Conway set up lavender plantation there. Original plan: distillation of aromatic plants for extraction of chemical oils, also spirit from potatoes. 20 acres of lavender stretched nearly to Henley; 100 women and children employed. Druids' Temple built at Park Place from 45 stones brought from prehistoric burial ground in Jersey (1785). Garden mentioned in Horace Walpole's *Hieroglyphic Tales. (291,299,310)*
Berkshire Militia formed. *(89)*
Peat pits near Newbury for 16 miles; 1-2ft deep, quarter to half mile wide. Bones of deer, horns of antelope, remains of boars and beavers found. No acorns, but many fir cones. *(310)*

1759. Windsor Forest Turnpike Trust formed to remedy appalling state of road from Sonning to Virginia Water. Three toll gates. Many roads in disgraceful state. A329 follows approximate route of this new road. *(294,415)*
Hannah Snell married at Newbury. She had served as a dragoon in the Army and also in the Navy. Her sex passed unnoticed. Died 1792, an inmate of Chelsea Hospital, where she is buried. *(89)*

1760. First Enclosure Acts. *(471)*
Maidenhead growing popular as first stop on a journey to the West. Mrs Philip Lybbe Powys wrote: 'Our first place of breakfasting was the Orkney Arms, Maidenhead Bridge' (see 1743). *(57)*

1761. Reading population estimated at 8,000. *(289)*
Capability Brown laid out grounds of Caversham Park for Lord Cadogan. *(291)*

1762. William Augustus, 1st Duke of Cumberland, 2nd son of George II, headed first official list of racing colours allocated by the Jockey Club. He founded training stables at Kate's Gore near Ilsley. He bred the legendary Eclipse (never beaten) at Cranbourne Lodge, Windsor (1764), where he had first and most valuable stud in England. This was the beginning of serious training at Lambourne. Smith's Lawn (Windsor Polo Ground) named after his Horse Master. The Ascot course began to wane in popularity and the Duke decided to revitalise it. *(171,307,308, 226)*
Thomas Clack, inn-keeper of the Lamb, Wallingford, had three beautiful daughters. On 7 May Frances married William, 2nd Viscount Courtney. Had 13 daughters and one son (3rd Viscount). Another daughter married Sir John Honeywood Bt, of Kent. *(157)*

1763. Bradfield Hall built for the Hon John Barrington, natural son of George II. His successor (1811) built the almshouses. *(291)*

1766. Newbury riots over high bread prices. *(91)*

1768. On death of Sir Mark Pleydell, the Manor of Coleshill and newly-built manor house which his wife had inherited passed to his grandson, 2nd Earl of Radnor. Sir Mark's only daughter had married William Bouverie, Viscount Folkestone, who was created Earl Radnor in 1765. Their son assumed name 'Pleydell' in addition to his own. Pleydell-Bouverie family remained lords of manor until 1945. Bouverie family came from Flanders, when Laurence des Bouveries and wife settled in Canterbury (1568). *(291)*

Rebellion at Eton College over the right of assistant masters to send back to college those found out of bounds; 160 boys were involved. They 'took boats' and went to Maidenhead to stay in Marsh's Inn near the bridge. Among them was William Grenville (in 1806-7 as Whig statesman presided over the 'All The Talents' coalition). *(57)*

1769. Present Newbury Bridge begun. *(91)*

Edward Vansittart born. Became rector of Taplow. Added name 'Neal' to Vansittart. Family lived at Bisham Abbey, had connections with Oliver Cromwell and Lawrence of Arabia. His second marriage to Anne Spooner (1780-1873). Their great-nephew, the Rev William Archibald Spooner (1844-1930), the 'spoonerism' parson. Anne's sister Barbara married William Wilberforce, leader of anti-slave trade campaign. *(78)*

St Peter's Church, Wallingford, destroyed in Civil War, rebuilt by Robert Taylor, a gothic version of Wren's St Bride's. Bridge House next door also by Taylor. Castle Priory House home of Sir William Blackstone (1723-80) (see 1749), instrumental in bringing turnpike roads from Oxford and Wantage through Wallingford to revive its prosperity. Buried in St Peter's. *(299)*

1770. John Stair, schoolmaster of Aldermaston, produced the first William Pear. *(471)*

Road made from Ascot Heath to Reading through common and forest. It became a highwaymen's run. Bracknell grew up from the inns on it.

1771. Culham Court, Remenham, built. *(299)*

1772. By this date, Reading cloth trade had seriously declined. Widespread poverty and unemployment. A major factor was northern competition. *(114)*

Duke of Cumberland introduced cup at Ascot Races, which became the Gold Cup. He began the revival of Royal Ascot. *(171)*

1773. Maidenhead Cricket Club founded (see 1793). First cricket in county played at Oldfield, Bray, a former archery ground. *(58)*

Madam Crew (Frances Anne, daughter of Fulke Grenville) moved to Braywick House. She stayed until 1775. Fashionable hostess. Her parties included Charles Fox, Edmund Burke, R.B. Sheridan (see 1969). *(64)*

Dr Henry Wilder, rector of Sulham, bought Purley Hall (see 1609). Later let it to Warren Hastings, former Governor General of India, during long trial for alleged corruption (Hastings acquitted with honour). *(291)*

1774. Hungerford became first town to obtain free delivery of letters from post office. *(298)*

1775. Present Buckland House built for Roman Catholic family of Throckmorton. Ashes of Knight of Kerry here. Magnificent park. Thomas, son of Geoffrey Chaucer, once held the manor. Original grant 1229 to Hugo de Bolland. *(291,299)*

Benham House, Stockcross, home of Sutton family until 1939-45 war, when US servicemen moved in. Sir Richard Sutton built much of village. *(291)*

1776. Turnpike road Newbury to Oxford open. *(226)*

1777. Bulmershe Court, Earley, built. *(299)*

Maidenhead Bridge, designed by Sir Robert Taylor (he designed Lincoln's Inn), opened. Corporation borrowed £19,000 to pay for it. Collected £120,000 in tolls over the years but never repaid the debt. *(58)*

At old cock-pit at the Marquis of Granby's Head, Windsor, contest called a main of cocks between gentlemen of Berks and Oxon opened. Fighting for four days; 31 cocks each side for 5 guineas a battle and 100 guineas the odd battle. *(189)*

First Sunday School held by the Rev Thomas Stock at Ashbury Church. Sarsen stones west side of churchyard said to be part of mystic circle which once surrounded the village. *(291)*

1778. George III took up residence at Windsor. He walked about town, an amiable figure; everyone knew him and he knew everyone. Children would not stop for him when playing in the park and he would stand and watch them for as long as half an hour. When Eton boys dressed up for their Montem at Salt Hill, Slough, he was there with 50 guineas in his hand for them. George III first royal resident in Windsor for 50 years. He began royal farms, used Windsor shops (see 1793). *(171)*

1780. Inoculation against smallpox at Newbury (see 1753). *(89)*

Main arch of Abingdon Bridge widened. *(38)*

Parishioners paying tithes to Vicar of Cumnor entertained on Christmas afternoon with 4 bushels of malt brewed into ale, 2 bushels of wheat made into bread and half hundredweight of cheese. Parish one of largest in Berks until about this date. *(310)*

Fire swept down High Street, Drayton, destroying thatched cottages. Village raised £3,066 5s 9½d, paid 15 per cent of losses and built five almshouses for £283 18s 9d. Still there. Drayton famous for its walnut trees. *(291)*

Present Faringdon House (see 1645) built by Henry James Pye, 'most feeble of the poet laureates'. His ode on George III's birthday immortalised in parody *Sing a Song of Sixpence*: 'And when the pie [Pye] was opened...' Headless ghost of Hampden Pye (Hamilton Tighe of *Ingoldsby Legends)* walks north wall (some say) of Faringdon Church. *(292,396)*

Buscot House in the Vale built. Contains famous *Briar Rose* series of Burn Jones's paintings. Burn Jones was staying at nearby Kelmscott with William Morris when 1st Lord Faringdon commissioned him. *(292,299)*

George Vansittart, sixth son of Anthony Vansittart of Shottesbrooke House, educated Reading School, bought Bisham Abbey on return from East Indies. Was member of Council of Bengal and Persian interpreter in the Persian and Bengalese Translators' Office. Became High Steward of Maidenhead (1794), MP for Reading, Captain of Maidenhead Infantry Association, died 1825. Three brothers, Henry, George, Robert, all members of Sir Francis Dashwood's Hell Fire Club (at Medmenham). Henry, governor of Bengal, sent Robert, a Persian mare, two elephants and a rhinoceros. Robert sent them to George III. *(78)*

Introduction of threshing machines at Mortimer caused alarm and wrecking of machines. Workers thought they would lose their jobs. Three leaders executed, three deported. *(89)*

1781. Arthur Benoni Evans, scholar, author, artist, grandfather of Sir Arthur Evans, archaeologist, born Compton Beauchamp.

Dr Richard Valpy head of Reading School until 1830, 'a mighty flogger' nicknamed 'Dr Wackerbach'. Made school known throughout England. Rebuilt it at his own expense (1790). Formerly in depressed state. He stood by with cane while boys drank ½pint watered milk and ate single slice of bread: their breakfast after 3 hours' study. His school books, especially his grammars, achieved wide popularity. His adaptation of Shakespeare's *King John* performed at Covent Garden 1803. Publications include *Greek Grammar* and *Latin Grammar* (both 1809). His second son, Abraham John, became editor and publisher. Began *The Classical Journal,* also published *The Pamphleteer. (101,114,125,126, 303)*

1782. Irish peer, Earl of Barrymore, moved to Wargrave. Built elaborate theatre there. Installed Delphini of Covent Garden as permanent clown. Gala opening night (1791) attended by George IV and nobility. London actors on stage. This and other ventures, on which he spent £300,000, broke him. Died in accident while escorting French prisoners to Dover (1793), heavily in debt. Sir Morris Ximenes, who commanded Wargrave Rangers in Peninsular War (1808-14), bought local cottages for 12 survivors of the accident. Barrymore was buried on Sunday, so his body could not be snatched for debt. *(336,373)*

1784. Mr Rose, brewer of Kingston, killed in duel with noted Dick England at Ascot Races. *(308)*

Palmer's New Mail Coaches left London (Monday 8 am) for Bath (Wednesday 11 pm). Newbury half-way. At George and Pelican, Speenhamland, three fours changed in less than an hour. This was first regular mail run in England (see 1784, 1832). *(89)*

Joseph Radley, highwayman - he was under 18 - executed after 30 holdups, including robbing two ladies and three gentlemen between Twyford and Reading (£5 5s), a Quaker in post chaise (watch and £3 3s), two foreigners in post chaise (£16 6s), four officers in post chaise £19 9s), two ladies (watch, gold seal, small picture, ring and £1 1s). *(494)*

1785. W.B. Simonds brewery founded, Broad Street, Reading. Moved to Bridge Street (1790) to site of dyeing house, which had been in use since 1221. *(1144,126)*

Wallingford Congregational chapel built. It eventually became Roman Catholic chapel. *(299)*

John Cooke became Maidenhead Congregational Minister. These were rough days for breakaway religions; crowds attacked him with lighted straw dipped in pitch. He objected to strolling players and was involved in vitriolic pamphlet war. *(58,88)*

1786. Reading workmen dug up box containing embalmed hand. Presented to Reading Museum. Lewis Mackenzie bought it for £30. Acquired from his brother by Scott Murray of Danefield of Great Marlow, who gave it to the Roman Catholic Church of St Peter, Marlow. Believed to be hand of St James (beheaded AD 44, hand struck off, body preserved in Cathedral of Santiago de Compostella) (see 1125). *(102,231)*

Mr Broom of Kennington sold his wife for five shillings to Littlemore man called Pantin, who led her away with halter round her neck, but later gave her to the woodman of Bagley Woods. *(291)*

Sunday schools established in Newbury.

William Herschel (1738-1822), British astronomer, moved to Slough, having lived in Windsor and Datchet. Discovered planet Uranus (1781) and several of its satellites. Astronomer to George III from 1782. At his Slough observatory, discovered infra-red solar rays (1800). Built giant telescope at Observatory House, Slough. George III and Archbishop of Canterbury walked through the tube before the lenses were fitted. First president of Royal Astronomical Society. He began space discovery. For his successors, see 1960 & 1973. *(303,428)*

John Steptoe executed at Reading for sheep stealing.

John Walter (1739-1812) acquired printing office on Blackfriars and started *Daily Universal Register.* Re-named it *The Times* (1788). His son William transferred the business to his younger brother John Walter (1766-1847) who built reputation of *The Times.* John Walter the 3rd (1818-1894) and descendants continued with it. John Walter the First began as coal merchant. Family lived at Farley Hill Place and Bear Wood. *(299,502)*

1787. Eight mail coaches a day over Maidenhead Bridge. *(57)*

George III and royal family attended Maidenhead Races. *(58)*

Morgan Jones (or Blewbury Jones the Miser), vicar of Blewbury, was original of Blackberry Jones in Dickens' *Our Mutual Friend.* Jones left 1824. Church contains memorial brass to Sir John Daunce, surveyor to Henry VIII. *(291)*

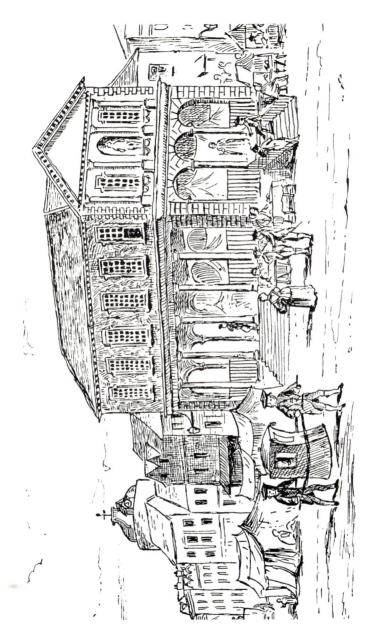

Windsor Guildhall sketched in 1770. (RS)

xvii

LETTER V.

To the HIGH PRIEST of the Tabernacle in the CITY of the VIRGIN.

YE, who the Gospel to your views expound,
By fools thought learned, and by few thought sound;
Who charity, and social bonds despise—
Hell's in your hearts! and Sion in your eyes!
Whose saintly looks and sable vestments hide
The filth and nastiness conceal'd inside.
In vain ye rave; so frantic in your spite—
I'll drag your works of darkness into light;
And brandish o'er your backs th' AVENGING ROD,
Who, fed by Mammon, teach the flock of GOD!!!
Explaining as ye list the Heavenly Book,
Till SION's SHEPHERD turns to *Satan's Cook*;
And feeds his flock with Gospel till they're fit,
And serves up SION's SHEEP at *Satan's spit*.

ABOVE: 17th century Maidenhead noncomformist calumnies.
BELOW: Cliefden House, Maidenhead in the 18th century.

xviii

1788. Temple Mills, Bisham, rolling copper sheets, making bolts for Royal Navy and copper bottoms for distilleries.

1789. James Cocks founded Reading Sauce Factory. By 1814 Cocks' Reading Sauce was well-known throughout the kingdom. *(126)*

John Elwes, the Marcham miser, died. (Great grandson of Dean Meggott, who bought the Marcham estate.) Became one of best riders in Europe. Built Portland Place, Portman Square and great part of Marylebone. Sat as MP, never spoke. *(303)*

After teaching Duke of Marlborough's children writing, William Fordyce Mavor made vicar of Hurley by Duke; LLD conferred same year. Mavor invented system of shorthand. Published *Universal Stenography* (1779). Wrote some 40 books, including *General View of Agriculture of Berkshire. (303)*

1790. Hurley Lock built.

1791. Windsor Great Park became George III's interest. Norfolk Farm 1,000 acres. Flemish Farm 400 acres (named from nature of husbandry), rest plantation and park. Large-scale improvements to create employment for industrious poor, 180 oxen worked in trams of six; 200 kept; 40 fattened annually. *(310)*

1792. Book of deeds relating to Reading Abbey properties found at Shinfield. Now in British Museum. *(291)*

George III attended first army manoeuvres in heathlands at Sandhurst. Led to building of Royal Military Academy. *(291,373)*

1793. Windsor Theatre Royal opened in High Street. (In Queen Anne's day, theatrical performances were given in the original Duke's Head, Peascod Street, also at a hall in Sheet Street.) The manager was Mr Thornton. There was a royal box and six fiddlers. George III and his Queen attended twice a week. The King bowed to the audience in the tiny theatre, to which he and his entourage often walked. George III loved the comedies and farces, laughing heartily at them. Coffee was handed round the court circle. Building became dissenters' chapel; playgoers raised fund to replace it (see 1832). *(171,374)*

Maidenhead Cricket Club defeated MCC at Lords, playing for 500 guineas a side. (Maidenhead team of 18 defeated all-England XI in (1835). *(58)*

Lord Bruce wrote to his father, the Earl of Aylesbury, that Lord Elgin had most fortunate escape from footpads who attacked him on Maidenhead Thicket.'That serves as a lesson not to travel by night in our country.' *(57)*

Reading County Gaol built. Old Castle Street prison (for both sexes) condemned by prison reformer John Howard. It had treadmill that public could watch. *(101,472,474)*

1794. Reading population estimated at 8,500. *(289)*

East Ilsley sheep market, second in size to Smithfield (see 1750), penned 80,000 sheep in a day, of which 50,000 were sold. Annual average 400,000 of Hampshire Cotswold and Leicester breeds. Held large wool fair in July. *(226)*

Berkshire Agricultural Society founded. Its plan to improve agriculture failed because it was turned into an electioneering movement. *(310,384)*
Act incorporating Kennet & Avon Canal Navigation Company. Management in hands of 'most respectable gentlemen and clergy of the different districts'. Navigation promoted by Acts of 1794, 1796, 1805 and 1813. *(278,279,280)*

1795. Infantry barracks for 1,000 troops built Sheet Street, Windsor (1795-1803). Pitt began policy of segregating troops in barracks for political reasons. *(18)*
Thomas Noon Talfourd born Reading (father one of Reading's 21 brewers). Friend and biographer of Charles Lamb. Reading MP (Liberal), fathered Copyright Act (1842). Friend of Dickens, who dedicated *Pickwick Papers* to him. Invited Dickens to stand as MP for Reading (1841). Talfourd resigned 1849. *(111,114,121)*
House in Rose Street, Wokingham, bought and used for Maiden School. *(219)*
Reading's Volunteer force put down rioting involving Irish troops stationed in town. Volunteers originally raised to keep order and be on standby for French invasion. Many troops passed through town during revolutionary and Napoleonic wars. Five pubs used as recruiting stations. *(126)*

20 MAY. Cliveden House, Taplow, destroyed by fire. *(63)*
Berks magistrates met at George and Pelican, Speenhamland, and invented notorious Speenhamland system of subsidising wages out of parish rates, which made farm labourers in work paupers. System adopted nationally. It lasted nearly 40 years. *(91,293)*

1797. Alarm over war in France. Newbury Volunteer Cavalry formed for protection of town and neighbourhood. *(89)*
First section of Kennet and Avon Canal opened, Newbury to Kintbury, 6 miles. 60-ton barge sailed at noon with 15th Regiment of Dragoons on board. Arrived 2.30. Canal reached Great Bedwyn 1799 (see 1723, 1810). *(273,274,278,279,280)*

1798. Kennet and Avon, 40ft wide, taking barges up to 110 tons. Object: to carry household and smiths' coal from Gloucestershire and Somerset mines, stone coal for maltsters from South Wales, Bath stone for building and to open market for Berks grain and timber. Completed circuit of navigable canals traversing northern midlands, south western counties and the four largest rivers: Trent, Mersey, Severn, Thames. K & A Canal became central line of communication between Irish Sea and German Ocean. *(208)*
At Ascot race-week breakfast, a 'new attraction' on show: a billiards table. This was its first appearance in Berkshire. *(310)*

1799. Wallingford Congregationalists opened chapel. They previously held services in town hall (see 1881). *(162,333)*

Nineteenth Century

When the nineteenth century began Berkshire was a rural county. The stage coach era was at its height. There was no organised police force, fire brigade, piped water, hospitals, or general suffrage for ratepayers. When it ended, the energy and enterprise of the Victorians had transformed the towns, created High Street shopping, and brought a form of social security into existence which had been unheard of until they arrived. But even so, vagrancy was the scandal of the age. In spite of their enormous energy, their efforts, with some notable exceptions, stopped short of the lower classes.

The prelude to the industrial age in Berkshire was the serious riots over the introduction of farm machinery at Newbury. But the greatest influence for change was steam which brought the Great Western Railway, and ended coaching and water transport.

Victorian shop-keepers took over the work started by the ancient guilds. They set up police forces to protect their property, hospitals and dispensaries to keep their work people fit. Reading, which suffered typhus epidemics and occasional cases of cholera – its back streets were full of stagnant pools – was a particularly unhealthy place. Infant mortality in the county was exceptionally high.

It was the Victorians who laid the foundations of Reading University, which in this agricultural county had a strong bias towards husbandry, and they started the Workers' Educational Association in Reading.

Berkshire became a royal county when Windsor Castle became the country seat of the monarch. Nationally, new local government Acts in the 1890s brought into existence, county, rural, district, urban and parish councils, which gave rural areas elected representation for the first time.

The shop-keepers provided the mayors and the aldermen, who in the main set out to run town affairs as economically as possible to keep down taxes. The boroughs were self-reliant places resenting interference from outside. Victorian society became well-organised with clear cut class distinctions and it was their prosperous trading which brought about the stability of a gradually enlarging middle class, which was to become a stabilising influence in the country.

1800. Cavalry barracks, Windsor, first built. Occupied by Blues 1804. Reconstructed 1865-70. Renamed Combermere 1900. *(189)*
About this time, Reading began a piped water supply through elm pipes. Mill Lane pumping station sent water to tank in Broad Street for distribution to some houses through lead pipes. Pipes sometimes blocked by fish. *(126)*
Abingdon pioneered the use of jute for carpet making. *(38)*
Edward Bouverie Pusey born. His father, Viscount Folkestone, adopted name Pusey (1789) when succeeded to Pusey estate. Edward became Regius Professor of Hebrew, Oxford, and Canon of Christ Church. With brother Philip and Dr Ellerton, founded the Pusey and Ellerton Hebrew

scholarships. Philip (1799-1855) also prominent agriculturalist (see 1840). *(303)*

Newbury paved and lighted by public subscription: £1,140 raised in a morning for this venture. *(310)*

1801. Population Act gave Reading's population as 9,742. Berks: inhabited houses 20,573; uninhabited 622; population 109,215 (male 52,821, female 56,394); 38,155 in agriculture; 16,921 in manufacturing and handicrafts. *(289)*

Hop cultivation in decline; formerly considerable. Now largest acreage at Faringdon (10), Bisham (2), Hurley, Bradfield. *(310)*

Henry Addington (1757-1854) Tory Prime Minister (1802-4), created Viscount Sidmouth (1805). Son of Reading doctor. Presented land on which Royal Berks Hospital built (see 1839). *(114)*

Rev Wyatt Cottle, vicar of Cholsey (1801-32), honeymooned at Mount Lebanon. His wife smuggled seedling cedars home in her parasol. They still grow in the churchyard. *(291)*

20 DEC. Annual bull-baiting day at Wokingham. Sermon previous day on the barbarity of it. *(220)*

1802. Tom Stuchbery joined his uncle in Maidenhead grocery business. Stuchberys a Bucks brewing family; Tom taught Robert Nicholson to brew beer. William Nicholson (b1820) started Pineapple Brewery. Grew into Nicholson's brewery, now part of Courage brewing empire. At about this time the families of Stuchbery, Nicholson, Webber (draper) and Budgen (grocer) were creating Maidenhead's High Street. *(58)*

Further improvements to Kennet Navigation. With opening of canal, produce of Ireland and West Indian settlements passed along it to Reading.

Roman Catholic tradition began in Reading. *(126)*

Reading Dispensary founded by Richard Oliver, a Roman Catholic. Royal Berkshire Hospital succeeded it. *(126)*

Newbury Old Theatre built. Unique ceiling; part remains. *(91)*

Thomas Huntley, of the Huntley & Palmer partnership, rented his first shop from Cocks who lived next door (see 1789). *(121)*

1803. At Maidenhead, 140 inhabitants sworn in as 'specials' to meet threat of French invasion. Similar forces in being in other parts. In Newbury, gentlemen joined the Mounted Association. *(57,58)*

1805. Berkshire Militia Battalion formed. Raised as a sort of local defence force. The colour presented by the commanding officer, Major-General George Henry Vansittart, and laid up in Bisham Abbey, when the battalion was disbanded (1814), is still there. *(78,87)*

Whole Volunteer Corps of Berkshire reviewed on Maidenhead Thicket in deep snow by the Duke of Cambridge. *(494)*

1806. John Sutton opened as corn and seed merchant in Reading Market Place. Supplied Royal Farms at Windsor and the Duke of Marlborough, who was turning 80 acres of Whiteknights into ornamental park. *(114)* John Younge Akerman born at Abingdon (1806-1873). Became numismatist and antiquary and secretary to William Cobbett and of the Society of Antiquaries. Popularised study of coins in England. Published many papers on antiques and coins, particularly a *Descriptive Catalogue of Rare and Unedited Roman Coins* (2 volumes), *Coins of the Romans relating to Britain, Ancient coins of Cities and Princes,* etc. Awarded gold medal of the French Institute for the above. *(303)*

1808. Martha May (55) died at Wokingham. She was hurt by fighters after bull-baiting. The Wokingham Fighters, a body of roughs, were notorious for picking quarrels. Fights took place at the Cockpit, often witnessed by members of the council. *(219,221)*

1809. Water carriage of goods now amounted to half land carriage. Barge from Abingdon took 5 days to London and 10 days to return. Because of Thames navigation uncertainties, Faringdon hogs sent by waggon. Navigational aids neglected. Perishable articles not entrusted to river. Thames and Severn Canal had little trade; Berks and Wilts Canal through the Vale 'more use to public than proprietors'. Navigation toll on Thames 3d per ton at each pound lock. Tonnage in 1801, a peak year, was 777,920. *(294,310)*

Major repairs to Wallingford Bridge by John Treacher. He replaced mediaeval arches. *(157,159,161,162)*

Mavor reported on state of agriculture and industry in county. Wokingham: 3 silk manufacturers, one for spinning, two for weaving hatbands, ribbons, watchstraps, shoestrings, sarsnets (for linings), figured gauzes. Spinning and twisting mill (432 spindles) worked by one horse; about 100 of all ages employed. Reading: pin manufactory, weaving of braid, satin, ribbon and light fabrics. Floor cloth made, sent to London for painting; sail making, twine and rope making. Wallingford: 16 or 17 malt houses. Brown malt dried with beech millet, pale with coke and cinders. Mr Well's brewery largest in county. Small sacking manufactory. Large quantities of sacking and hammocks for government. Ten principle masters in hemp manufacture, five making light 'foulweather' cloth for labouring poor. Mr Sylvester's tan yard largest in kingdom. Proprietor, Mr Desmond, assisted by German in new art of tanning. Oak bark has greatest amount of tannin, hence necessity of cultivating it for timber and bark. Windsor: some children employed in poor house, making straw hats. Ramsbottom's brewery made Queen's Ale; Jenning's, King's Ale. Newbury: woollen manufacture nearly lost, numerous poor, but kerseys (coarse cloth), cotton callicoes, linen and damask manufactued. Many barges built for carrying timber to London. Maidenhead: malting for London market, small sacking manufactured cotton mills at Taplow employed Maidenhead boys and girls. Hungerford: women span serge; Faringdon: worsted. *(310)*

Wantage one of cheapest towns in country: beef and mutton averaged 7d lb, lamb 7½d. Faringdon and Reading 1d a lb dearer. Berkshire cheese between 6d & 7d lb, butter 1s to 1s 6d. 'Cheese in great measure supplies the place of meat to the labourer.' Butter only a luxury. Wokingham celebrated for fatted fowl, its principal commerce, at 15s a couple. *(310)*

In eastern Berks, many geese reared on commons. Few bees kept by higher classes, but Sir William East of Hall Place, Hurley, had long been celebrated apiarist. Berkshire hogs usually crossed with Chinese or Tonquin race, in 6 or 7 generations with Indian race. About 4,000 slaughtered at Faringdon, Michaelmas and April; one of principal markets in kingdom. 'Several rich capitalists dealing in bacon and cheese' at Faringdon. Native breed of sheep Berkshire Notts. Great size and height on legs, and weight when fattened. Pack of short wool £15. Eight fleeces to a tod of wool (usually 28lbs). At Ilsley Fair 30,000 sheep sold. *(310)*

Queen Charlotte, the Duke of Cambridge and the Princesses Augusta, Sophia, Elizabeth and Mary taken by boat from Maidenhead Bridge to Cliveden, where they were received by Lady Orkney. Crowds lined the banks. *(57)*

Berks landed property estimated worth £500,000 pa. Great Landowners rare. Earl of Craven held largest possessions among peers, E.L. Loveden Esq among commoners. Greatest income about £8,000 pa. Respectable number of high-spirited yeomanry actively engaged in agriculture was distinguishing mark of county. Old families: Cravens, Englefields, Eystons, Reades, Southbys, Seymours, Clarkes. Old families on female line: Berties, Nevilles, Playdells, Puseys, Throckmortons, Lovedens, Nelsons, Blagraves. 'Proudest rank country gentleman can hold, to live on his estates and to diffuse happiness around him . . . the father of his dependents and to grow old among them.' *(310)*

Agricultural crops: Vale of White Horse had abundant crops of wheat and beans; chalk district hills covered with sheep; in east, turnips, barley, lammas wheat, artificial grasses; Vale of Kennet had lammas wheat, turnips, barley. Dr Beeke, rector of Ufton and professor of modern history at Oxford University, reported county covered 461,500 acres; arable 255,000, meadows and dairy land in Vale 72,000, sheep walks on chalk hills 25,000, dry pastures and parks 25,000, wastes (barren heaths) 30,000, woods and copses 30,000, buildings, roads, fences, rivers etc 27,500. House of Lords Report (1805) estimated 476,160 acres (744 square miles) and 147 persons to square mile.

Fish in Thames: barbel, pike, trout, eels (excellent quality), gudgeon, dace and various other common fish (exclusive of carp and tench, probably brought in by floods). Average price of Thames fish 1s per lb. Kennet: 'swift for silver eels renown'd', also trout (they have reached 45 inches), barbel, pike, crayfish, chub, roach and dace. The Lodden: 'slow with verdant alders crowned' was subject of Pope's *Fable of Ladona*. *(310)*

Between July and November, Thames short of water for navigation from Wallingford to Windsor. No pen, lock or staunch below Windsor (a distance of 29 miles) to obtain navigable depth of even 3ft: whole of water penned by locks between Windsor and Reading, run for 12 to 14 hours Thursdays and Sundays, at time of year when it ought to have been husbanded for mills and navigation. Sometimes the 'flash' of water carried the barges to Windsor and sometimes it did not. Plan for canal from Maidenhead to join Grand Junction at Cowley to reduce distance from Reading to London by barge to 59½ miles. *(284,310)*

4,000 shares in Kennet and Avon Canal issued at £24 a share. By September, price went to £46-49 and by January 1810 to £50 (see 1948). *(280)*

'The increasing expenses of labour, which, however, is still inadequate to the support of those who are engaged in agriculture, would deserve to be considered as a drawback on improvements, were not the poor rates proportionally diminished by the allowance made to the labouring cultivator of the soil'. Wages: Biscuit bagging (Abingdon) men 18s - 20s; women 5s; children 1s 6d-2s 6d. Agricultural labourer 9s (increased by one fourth in past ten years but inadequate to support family without driving a man to the parish for assistance on every emergency). Silk manufacture (Wokingham) men 30s; women 8s-10s; children 5s. Floor cloth, sail twine, rope making (Reading) men 15s-25s; women 6s-10s. *(310)*

1810. Wilts and Berks Canal opened (Abingdon to Kennet and Avon link at Semington). Branches to Chippenham, Wantage and Longcot. Kennet and Avon Canal opened. Cost approximately £1m, length 57 miles, 79 locks, 2 viaducts, one tunnel. Now continuous waterway for barges from London to Bristol. It transported coal, iron, salt, grain, sugar, tea, timber, bricks and building stone for 40 years. *(294)*

1811. John Hibbert of Braywick Lodge, Maidenhead, born (d1888). Helped to establish Windsor Hospital, of which he became chief benefactor; also a prime mover in setting up Maidenhead Cottage Hospital. *(58)*

John Coxeter of Greenham Mills (100 hands) won bet of 1,000 guineas from Sir John Throckmorton that between sunrise and sunset he could make a coat from wool that was growing on a sheep's back. At 5 am on 25 June, Sir John and shepherd presented two fat Southdown sheep. Shorn, the wool was washed, stabbed, roved, spun and woven. Cloth was scoured, dyed and dressed by 4 pm. James White, tailor of Newbury, cut coat. Nine men with needles threaded took the cloth and completed the coat by 6.20 pm. Bet was accepted to demonstrate efficiency of the mill. Throckmortons at Buckland Manor since 1690. (Buckland House is now University Hall.) *(89,98,292)*

All Saints' Church, Abingdon (built by monks c.1480) rebuilt by 3rd Earl of Abingdon, who demolished Cumnor Place. East window said to be from Amy Robsart's room. *(35,38)*

Reading's trade increased. Population up to 10,800 from 9,400. *(126)*

1812. From this date Wallingford ran a local penny post service to Benson, Shillingford and Dorchester. The GPO was only responsible for the carriage of post to the post town. Some local postmasters ran private delivery and collection services, charging about a penny. At Maidenhead, Lord Boston of Hedsor Lodge tried to get an official penny post for the Maidenhead area (1814), but Mrs Winder, the local postmistress, had her own local arrangement, which she did not want upset (see 1830). *(162)*

Mary Russell Mitford and her parents moved to Three Mile Cross from Bertram House, Grazely, because of Dr Mitford's gambling debts. Mary kept the impoverished family by writing for the *Lady,* laid foundations for new branch of literature and became famous. Mary (1787-1855) educated at Abbey Boarding School, Reading, which moved to Chelsea (name taken by present Abbey Girls' School), as was Jane Austen. Mitfords formerly lived next to Watlington House, Reading. Mary, at age 10, won £20,000 in lottery. She chose ticket No. 2224 (digits added to her age). Father built Reading house with cash and took to gambling in a big way. They ended up in 'Mr Body's cottage at the Cross'. Mary, a precocious child who once read 55 books in 31 days, wrote Three Mile Cross into *Our Village.* Became friendly with Lady Russell of Swallowfield (see 1820), where her carriage overturned. She lost the use of legs and arms and is buried behind Swallowfield Church. *(246-254)*

First issue of *Windsor & Eton Express & General Advertiser.* Charles Knight, founder and first editor, wrote: 'Royal Windsor ... country town of narrowest range of observation ... the people vegetated although living amidst a continual din of royalty ...' *(489)*

Reading National School founded; half boys, half girls. By 1814, 600 pupils. *(126)*

Annual Melon Feast, Windsor, arranged by the Society of Gentleman Gardeners at the Three Tunns.

1815. Stage coach era getting into its stride. Speedier travel for people and goods. Billingsgate fish on sale in Reading by 2 pm. *(126, 231-240)* Newbury Races on Enborne Heath. *(89,90)*

1816. Son of Reverend Fulwar Craven Fowle, incumbent of Kintbury for 40 years, described by George III as 'the best preacher and best rider to hounds in my whole county of Berkshire', engaged to Cassandra, Jane Austen's sister. *(291)*

William Plenty of Newbury invented lifeboat. Launched from West Mills and named *The Experiment.* Eighty people sailed up the Kennet and Avon Canal in her. Royal Naval Institution for the Preservation of Lives from Shipwreck ordered boats for coastal stations. Plenty also invented the Berkshire Iron Plough, which won the Duke of Bridgewater's Prize for a plough best adapted to all agricultural purposes. *(90)*

Cholsey's tithe barn, 51ft high, 54ft wide, 303ft long, pulled down. Tithes paid by farmers to abbots of Reading were stored there. *(43)*

French ship loaded with linen anchored off High Bridge, Reading. It was on cross-country voyage to Bristol. *(108,114,126)*

1817. William Douglas, beadle at Wokingham until 1831, received new coat and hat every three years. The office, a civil one, had been in existence in Wokingham since at least 1327, when John le Bedel held it. *(219)*

Father Longuet, Reading's Roman Catholic priest, mugged and murdered in Oxford Road. *(126)*

Holy Brook, Reading, fenced in. Within living memory, 101 children had drowned there. *(126)*

1818. Pascoe Grenfell bought Manor of Bray from the Crown. He also bought the Bray manors of Ive (1800) and Shoppenhangers (1801). This was a major change in landlordship from Crown to commoner. *(58)*
First primitive piped water supply for the well-off in Reading. It worked on Mondays, Wednesday, Fridays and Sundays only. *(114)*
Edward Hawke Locker published plan (1817) for a general dispensary in Windsor, because the poor could not afford medical care. His plan for a charitable medical service for the poor of Windsor, Eton and district was set up at a public meeting. Queen Charlotte, the Princesses Augusta, Elizabeth and Sophia and the Duke of York opened the subscription list. The volunteer medical staff included the Surgeon-Apothecary to George IV (and William IV), John O'Reilly. *(211)*
1820. 12 JAN. Francis Baily (1774-1844) one of 14 who founded Astronomical Society. An eminent astronomer, third son of Richard Baily, a banker of Newbury. Exposed Berenger Fraud (1814), wrote Stock Exchange investigation report and standard works on assurance. By his writing, also helped to speed astronomical progress. *(303)*
1820c. Richard Cox, Bermondsey brewer, retired to Colnbrook. There he raised the apple Cox's Pippin, which first fruited 1840 and was put on the market by Turner's Nursery, Slough. *(428)*
Cock-fighting popular at Long Wittenham. Site of pit near school. Mains fought between birds representing neighbouring counties. *(43)*
Mrs Dickinson, author of *Old Court Life in France* and friend of Miss Mitford (see 1812), lived at Farley Court. *(299)*
Sir Henry Russell bought Swallowfield Manor and entertained Dickens, Wilkie Collins, Thackeray, Charles Kingsley, Mary Mitford. Russell family lived there until 1965. *(414)*
1821. Last salmon caught in Thames at Maidenhead. *(58)*
Beginning of heyday of commercial water carriage. Upper Thames used since late 17th century, but Kennet & Avon canal now vital link in the southern half of the nationwide network. Regular service from Abingdon to Melksham (Wilts & Berks) by light boats pulled by fast horses. Abingdon also linked with midland coal fields and Bristol. *(274)*
Coronation of George IV and beginning of the Abingdon custom of throwing buns from the Town Hall to the waiting crowd below on special occasions. At Hungerford, £10 was voted to supply beer tickets for inhabitants wishing to drink His Majesty's health. *(35,54)*
William Cobbett visited Prosperous Farm, Hungerford, formerly owned by Jethro Tull. *(89)*
1822. Thomas Hughes born, author of *Tom Brown's Schooldays* (1856). Spent childhood at Uffington. Became QC, county court judge, MP for Lambeth and Frome. Grandson of Reverend Dr Hughes, preceptor in royal family of George III, one of the Clerks of the Closet to George II and George IV, Vicar of Uffington (1816-1833). Sir Walter Scott came to know area through the Hughes family. References in *Kenilworth,* including Weyland's Smithy. *(43,145,152,155)*
Mrs Martha Pye, aged 117, buried at Sutton Courtenay. *(291)*

1823. Highworth Coach ran to London three times a week from Wallingford. There were other daily coach services to Reading and Oxford. *(162)*

1824. Windsor's cast iron bridge opened. Consulting engineer was Thomas Telford. It became the setting for ceremonial entrances to Windsor. *(189)*

George IV began transformation of Windsor Castle into royal residence. Architect was Geoffrey Wyatt (known as Wyatville). *(189)*

Cliveden derelict until this year, when it was bought by Sir George Warrender and rebuilt (see 1795). *(63)*

1825. Hoard of gold found at Stanford. It had been hidden by villagers during the Civil War, so the story goes. *(43)*

National Schools built in Wokingham for 250 boys and girls. *(219)*

1825c. Copyright of George Canning's writings for *The Microcosm,* a publication founded by Canning and others while at Eton College, came into the possession of Charles Knight of Windsor. Work ran to five editions. Canning (1720-1827) succeeded Lord Liverpool as Prime Minister (1827). Lived at South Hill Park from about 1806. *(216)*

Abingdon Council began to use parts of old abbey as offices. *(38,47)*

1826. Boulters Lock, Maidenhead, worn out (see 1746) through heavy barge traffic: approximately 69,000 tons up stream annually. Barges 60ft long, towed by horses. *(58,271,272)*

1827. Building of Royal Berkshire Hospital began. Lord Sidmouth, son of local doctor, presented the land. Accidents during the building of Great Western Railway were to keep it busy. *(126)*

Newbury borough boundaries extended and Corporation acquired gas works. *(89,90)*

Lord Brougham founded in Reading the Society for the Diffusion of Useful Knowledge. It was satirised by novelist Thomas Love Peacock as the Steam Intellect Society. This and other societies and institutes led to the university extension movement and to the founding of the Workers' Educational Association. Forerunner of the extension movement in Reading was the government School of Science and Art; teachers came from South Kensington museums (see 1892). *(114,123,124)*

1828. Gas introduced into Windsor. *(189)*

Newbury guildhall (see 1611) demolished. *(90)*

Agricultural pioneer Philip Pusey of Pusey House helped form the Royal Agricultural Society of England. He turned Pusey Common into a North Berks show-place, with menagerie which included jackals, wolves, silver foxes and pheasants. Their food came on daily delivery from a Faringdon butcher. Disraeli described him as 'one of the most distinguished country gentlemen who ever sat in the House of Commons'.

Martin Sutton (John's son), aged 13, began buying and selling seeds. *(114)*

1828c. Newbury Market Cross demolished. *(90)*

Act for better watching, cleansing, paving and improving Wantage. Fires

and serious crimes had earned it the name of Black Wantage. *(163)*
Some 50 coaches a day travelling the Bath Road. Tickets booked at
London inns. Journey to Newbury took six hours. Coaches through
Maidenhead branched to both Abingdon and Wantage at the top of
Castle Hill. There were many famous names: Royal Defiance
(Abingdon), the Telegraph, Forest Coach (through Windsor Great
Park), New Post Coach (Staines and Sunninghill), the Accommodation,
all bound for Reading.) On the Bath run were the Royal Mail, the
Shamrock, the Blue (York House Company's coaches), the Regulator,
Post Coach, the Emerald, the Company's Day Coach and Night Coach
and the Triumph. (Two doors of the London & Bristol & Frome coaches
are preserved at Ferris's Motor Works, Newbury, and inscribed 'To
carry 4 inside and 11 out'.) *(231-240)*

1829. First Oxford and Cambridge Boat Race rowed at Henley-on-
Thames. Oxford crew trained on Berkshire reaches. *(58)*
New Boulters Lock built on Berks bank (see 1746, 1912). *(58,462)*
John Higgs founded Methodist Movement in Maidenhead. *(58,67)*
Punishments severe. In Reading, any theft above the value of 5
shillings meant hanging at Gallows Tree Common, Earley. There were
scores of other offences for which the punishment was death. *(126)*
Abingdon Bridge widened (see 1416). *(35,38,426)*
Henry Hart Milman, vicar of St Mary's, Reading, wrote renowned
History of the Jews. (114)

1830. Wallingford stocks last used. *(161)*
Farm machinery riots at Newbury (and in other parts). Farm workers
revolted against poor pay and the use of agricultural machinery. They
smashed machines, burned down barns, corn stalks and houses.
Government sent detachment of Grenadier Guards in express stage
coaches, followed by a troop of Lancers. The High Sheriff, Colonel
Dundas MP, ordered residents to muster on horseback. Party of 200 on
horse and on foot – Newbury Troop of Yeomanry, constables, horsemen,
Grenadiers and Lancers – moved on Kintbury, stronghold of the rebels.
High Sheriff also led a 'mounted column of gentlemen' against the
'discontented and disorderly peasantry'. Rebel groups holed up in inns,
stables and cottages. Red Lion and Blue Ball 'chief depots of these
enemies of public order'. The Sheriff's men moved to the Axe and
Compasses, Inkpen, then to West Woodhay and to Highclere. They took
100 prisoners to Newbury. Seventy committed for trial at special Assize
Court at Reading. In all, about 138 tried, all married and of previous good
character; 28 sentenced to death. A petition from Newbury for mercy
(950 signatures). Only one man, called Winterbourn, was executed.
Many deported for long periods. At Winchester Assizes, six sentenced to
death. *(89,383)*
Maidenhead adopted official penny post. 27,707 letters handled in one
year. *(298)*
Windsor began to grow, owing in part to the regular presence of the court
there. Its followers, including officials, servants and pensioners, called

for housing accommodation. Appropriately, the King's Road area began to expand. *(189)*

Vigorous moves at this time for Brunel's Great Western Railway. Brunel himself surveying parts of the route on horseback. The proposal met with opposition from vested interests and from, among others, the Headmaster of Eton College, Dr Hawtrey, who thought that the boys would truant to London by train and also that they would stone the trains passing by the college grounds. It was also reported that Queen Victoria disapproved of a railway line between the Castle and the Thames. *(199,241-245)*

1831. The Copper Horse, as it is known – George III statue – erected at Snow Hill at the top of Windsor Long Walk. *(189)*

Martin Sutton (see 1828) opened his first account with a wholesale seed house. *(114)*

Colonel Hippesley founded the West Berkshire Archery Club and initiated the 'York Round' (72 arrows at 100 yards; 48 at 80 yards; 24 at 60 yards). The club was limited to 12 members, who met to shoot the round. *(43)*

1832. Steam coaches made occasional appearances along the Bath Road. *(91)*

Until this year, the poor of Wantage received free bread on Lady Day. The custom had begun about 1786. *(163)*

Windsor Congregationalists, who had been meeting in the old Theatre Royal, opened their chapel in William Street and abandoned the theatre, the lease of which they had purchased (1807) and which they had used from the time that the lease expired (1813). Meanwhile, Windsor people had raised a fund for a new building, which went up in Thames Street, was burned down and the present building erected on the site. *(171)*

Saxon leg bone worked in gold and jewelled with garnets dug up at Milton. Now in Ashmolean Museum. *(291)*

1833. Great Western Railway's prospectus published.

Skindles Hotel, Maidenhead, founded by William Skindle (see 1914, 1918). *(231)*

Pork butcher of Thames Street, Windsor, fined for emptying pails full of filth from his 'blood hole' into the street. Another trader was similarly fined for allowing his pigs to run at large in Windsor Streets. *(189)*

1834. Poor Law Amendment Act passed. Boards of Guardians set up. Looked after workhouses and were responsible for their management. *(126)*

Windsor's Royal Dispensary moved to new building near Bachelors Acre, previously known as Pitt's Field, which was used for sporting events. *(211)*

Mr Dinorben Hughes arrived in Maidenhead to count the number of horse-drawn vehicles passing through the town. He had been commissioned by the Great Western Railway Company to appraise the railway's prospects. He reported that it was an important travel centre, with some 70 coaches and other through vehicles daily. *(242)*

1835. The Erin, a steam coach invented by Mr Hancock of Marlborough, now ran between Marlborough and London. It covered the 75 miles in 5 hours 48 minutes. Ogle & Sumner's steam coach also ran from Southampton to Oxford through Berks (see 1752,1834). *(89)*

William Henry Fox Talbot (1800-1877) produced the first photographic negative. He later set up processing laboratories in Reading. *(314,315)*

Municipal Corporations Act transferred the right to elect Corporation (of Reading etc) to the ratepayers. Previously Corporations had elected themselves. *(126)*

Maidenhead Gas Company founded. *(58)*

Although road communication had been improving steadily, often thanks to the turnpike trusts, of which there were 20 until this year, many roads were in a shocking condition. Through consolidation the trusts were reduced to 15 this year, but for instance, the road from Windsor to Reading through Twyford (present B3024), except in dry weather, was scarcely passable. *(192)*

John Sutton, Reading corn and seed merchant, exhibited tulips which were much admired. *(126)*

Newbury Union workhouse erected at cost of £5,000. It was feared by the poor. *(89,90)*

Fire at Bear Inn, Maidenhead. Thirty-five mail and coach horses died. One, called Miraculous, was saved and worked for some years on the Bristol Mail. The Bear was Maidenhead's principal inn in the coaching era. Travellers preferred to stay in Maidenhead overnight to risking attack and robbery on notorious Maidenhead Thicket at night. *(57,58, 231)*

No organised police force before this date in Windsor. A night constable and six watchmen were employed by the Improvement Commissioners to arrest vagrants and the disorderly. *(189)*

1836. Maidenhead appointed four constables, whose original duties were to apprehend beggars. They received half a crown for each one caught. *(290)*

George IV's transformation of Windsor Castle into a royal residence completed. *(58)*

One of the town's principal problems was to rid itself of the large number of beggars among a population of about 18,000. The policemen wore top hats. The Police Station was at 6 Friar Street, later moving to the Forbury (see 1855, 1857). *(115)*

Berkshire transferred to diocese of Oxford from province of Canterbury, diocese of Salisbury. *(219)*

Proposal to set up Reading police force of 34 at cost of £1,200 pa. For past seven years, town policed by night watchmen costing £493 7s 7d pa, beadles and street keepers costing £150 pa. The force came into existence on 21 February. The watchmen had been appointed by the Commissioners for Paving. *(115)*

Wallingford appointed three constables of the watch. They wore glazed hats and greatcoats and carried rattles, blunderbusses and pistols. *(162)*

63

1837. Daniel Gooch, aged 19, engaged by Isambard Kingdom Brunel (1806-1859) as chief locomotive assistant for Great Western Railway. He had designed two 6ft gauge locomotives for export to Russia, but they were never sent. One of them, the North Star, after which many pubs were to be named, was to pull the first Great Western Railway train. Delivered to Maidenhead by barge, where it remained until the permanent way reached the town in the following May. First of a great line of broad gauge locomotives for the Great Western Railway. *(241)* Martin Hope Sutton, son of John Sutton (see 1835), opened Suttons Seeds establishment in Reading and set the young firm on the road to becoming world famous. *(126)*

Building of the Sounding Arch, so-called because of the echoes created beneath it, began at Maidenhead. This was Brunel's famous bridge, having two of the flattest arches ever built in brickwork, each with a span of 128ft and a rise of only 24ft 3ins to the crown. *(58,241)*

First marriage in a non-conformist church in Reading. *(126)*

1838. Ufton Estate sold to Mr Benyon de Beauvon. *(291)*

4 JUNE. Great Western Railway opened from Paddington to Taplow. First train, pulled by North Star, carried 1,479 people and earned £226. A week later the trains were carrying road coaches on the last lap of their journey to London. Maidenhead (Riverside) station - it was at Taplow - was completed, with two clock towers reminding passengers that trains ran to Greenwich Mean Time. Local time throughout Berkshire varied: Maidenhead was 3 minutes behind Greenwich Mean Time. (A Miss Bellville of St Luke's Road, Maidenhead, used to distribute the time locally and to London firms with her chronometer, carrying on a business started by her father.) Thus the G. W. Railway spread   Greenwich Mean Time through Berkshire. There were large turnip pocket watches known as railway timepieces. Only two other stations besides Maidenhead - Euston and Birmingham - had raised platforms. Eton College, which prevented the railway going through Windsor, secured a clause in the Company's Act forbidding the erection of a station at Slough. The Great Western Railway hired two rooms in a pub by the track as a substitute. *(241-245)*

Chalmore Lock, Wallingford, built (removed 1838). *(162)*

1839. Great Western Railway opened to Twyford over Brunel's river bridge (the bridge immortalised in Turner's *Rain, Wind, and Steam,* National Gallery). Maidenhead Corporation, which had opposed the railway on the ground of loss of tolls, reduced toll on Maidenhead Bridge for a stage coach from £18 to £4. Bath Road inns began to feel the draught. At Salt Hill, Slough, where the opponents of the first Bill celebrated victory, the inns were to be virtually ruined. Smollett made them famous in *Humphrey Clinker,* mentioning the Salt Hill in where Matt Bramble, Tabitha and Miss Liddy dined on their way to London. *(241-245)*

Queen Victoria ordered the building of the Grand Stand at Royal Ascot, a year after she founded the Gold Vase. *(171)*

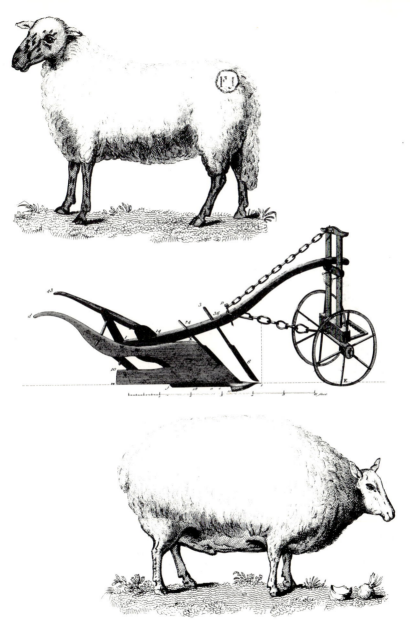

The Berkshire Nott Wether and a variant top and tail the Berkshire Common Plough - for
centuries, the county's sources of wealth.

West Berks Association

FOR THE PROSECUTION OF FELONS.

SIX
POUNDS
REWARD.

Whereas

During the Night of Monday, December the 21st, 1835, some person or persons stole

Seven Turkies

From a Fowl House at *Anville Farm*, near Hungerford, the property of Mr. WILLIAM CURNICK.

Whoever will discover the Offender or Offenders, shall on Conviction receive the Reward of £1 from Mr. Curnick, and £5 from the West Berks Association.

MATTHEWS and HULBERT,

Hungerford, Dec. 23rd, 1835.   Solicitors to the Association.

HALL AND MARSH, PRINTERS AND BOOKBINDERS, IMPERIAL PRESS, SPEENHAMLAND.

Quest for Hungerford fowl pests, 1835. (AP)

Royal Berkshire Hospital opened. The project had been backed by William IV. Prime mover was Richard Oliver (see 1802). Reading's public health in deplorable state and the town's conscience was roused. Cesspools contaminated drinking water; St Mary's gravedigger chopped up decomposing corpses to make room for victims of typhus and starvation. Cholera and typhus made town's death rate highest in the country: 37 in every 1,000. (There was no sponsored medical service until 1802.) Henry Addington (see 1801), whose home was Erlegh Court, gave the hospital site and Lady Sidmouth endowed it. *(114)*

Railway line cut at Shooters Hill, Pangbourne; 40 silver, gold and brass coins found, dating from AD 69-383, and many skeletons. *(291)*

Torrential rain hampered advance of Great Western Railway to Reading. Quagmire between Twyford and Sonning Cutting (60ft deep, 2 miles long). Two contractors abandoned the job and Brunel moved in with 1,220 navvies and 196 horses to move 24,500 cubic yards of spoil a week. *(241)*

1840. Great Western Railway reached Reading and the first train left Reading for London on 30 March. *(293)*

Christopher Smart married owner of the *Reading Mercury*, who founded first Roman Catholic Church in Reading since the Reformation. Built in Forbury Road on the spot where Hugh Faringdon, last Abbot of Reading Abbey, was hanged from 40ft gibbet. *(114)*

Whirlwind lifted 4-ton glass roof off newly-built Reading Station. William West, a glazier, killed. *(114)*

Radley Parish Church given collection of heraldic glass (15th and 16th centuries); best in Berkshire. Oak canopy in pulpit said to have hung over Speaker's chair in House of Commons.

Philip Pusey (1799-1855) (see 1800), took prominent part in the formation of what became, this year, the Royal Agricultural Society of England.

Whiteknights, the 18th century mansion (see 1292), pulled down and present gothic house built. The gardens, which were laid out in 1795, were the most famous in the South of England. *(299)*

Huntley, Bourne and Stevens founded. They made metal boxes for biscuits. *(121,126)*

Dr William Gordon Staples, of The Jungle, Ruscombe Road, Twyford, born. He was to become first 'gentleman gipsy'. *(291)*

Frederick Walker ARA born, lived in the Cookham area for a time. Painted *Harbour of Refuge* (Jesus Hospital, Bray), *Marlow Ferry*, *The Street, Cookham*, *The Fishmonger's Shop* etc. *(425,426)*

1841. Great Western Railway crash in Sonning Cutting. Nine passengers killed. *(241)*

National census showed that on average there were seven persons to a house in Windsor, that 15 out of every 100 children born there died in the first year, 32 before they were 5, 42 before they were 15. *(162)*

St Peter's Church, Knowl Hill consecrated. It was designed by J.C. Butler, runner-up to Sir Charles Barry in the competition for the design for the Houses of Parliament. *(291)*

George Palmer came to Reading and joined Thomas Huntley in his little shop at 72 London Road, where they began to make 'the Superior Reading Biscuits'. Both men were members of the Society of Friends. *(121)*

Windsor & Eton Choral Society formed. *(189)*

Roman milestone discovered in Six Acres Field, Finchampstead. Removed to Bannisters, a house which dates from 1683. *(240, 291)*

Charles Edward Appleton born. Educated Reading Grammar School, of which his father was headmaster. Founded literary periodical *Academy* (1869), editor until his death (1879). Organised movement for endowment of research. Men of eminence in literature and sciences contributed to *Academy*. Educational enthusiast. Became lecturer in philosophy at St John's, Oxford. *(303)*

1842. Henry Stevens became squarson (squire and parson) of Bradfield. Rebuilt 14th century church and opened choir school in what remained of Bradfield Place. He was also a pioneer in steam ploughing and milking machines. Began mineral water factory, helped reform Poor Law and established a workhouse. Bradfield is noted for its Blue Pool. *(291)*

1843. Stream of visiting royals, diplomats, statesmen and high society flowed into Windsor as the court spent more than half the year there.

1844. Act of Parliament annexed the district of Twyford to Berkshire; it was formerly included in Wiltshire. Old maps show it as 'part of Wiltshire'. It may have occurred because Sonning was part of the Manor of the Bishops of Salisbury. *(231)*

Slough signal box erected. One of first messages sent by its new electric telegraph was news of the birth of the Duke of Edinburgh. *(231,428)*

New Reading Gaol built, replacing condemned county gaol in Forbury. Oscar Wilde became a prisoner there and wrote, while a resident, *Ballad of Reading Gaol*. Designed by Sir George Gilbert Scott. *(114,126)*

Stage coaches from Reading to London ceased operation. The Great Western Railway had taken their business. Old coaching inns began to go into decline. The new coach-rail journeys begun by the Great Western Railway at Maidenhead were seen at Reading when the Duke of Wellington drove to the station from Stratfieldsaye in his coach. It was put on the train with the Duke inside it, to go to London. Successor to the coaching inn in Reading was the Great Western Hotel. *(126)*

Didcot junction opened (burned down 11 March 1851).

1845. John Tawell, who poisoned a woman at Salt Hill, escaped by train to Slough, unaware of the new electric telegraph. His description was sent to Paddington, where he was arrested and later hanged. First criminal to be caught by telephone. *(428)*

Maidenhead Congregationalists began British School at Maidenhead. *(58)*

Corn market began in Wantage to join older market for meat, butter, poultry, cheese and vegetables. *(43)*

Aldermaston Court burned down. It was built 1636 to replace previous house. Oak panelling and carving in the entrance hall and part of original staircase of 1636 (illustrated in Nash's *Mansions of Olden Times*) survived. Elizabeth, on two of her royal progresses through Berks (1558 and 1601), had stayed there. *(468,471)*

From this year all Wokingham was moved into Berks (see 1844). Previously part was in Wiltshire, including the parish church, the Manor of Ashridge (or Herstoke). *(219)*

Fox Talbot, pioneer of photography, had experimental laboratory in Baker Street, Reading (see 1835). *(114)*

William Legg, minister of Reading Congregational Church, quarrelled with congregation. He and his supporters left to found Trinity Congregational Church. They were called the 'Left Leggs'. *(126)*

Census of people crossing Windsor Bridge: estimated 649,411 in full year, with additional 35,000 in Ascot Week. *(189)*

1846. Crown consented to Great Western Railway branch line to Windsor from Slough and also to a South Western Railway proposal to link Windsor with Staines. The cash which the Crown received from the companies (£85,000) built new roads, bridges and improvements to the setting of the Castle. Earlier cost of improvements there had provoked a public outcry. A race to get to Windsor first began between the two companies (see 1849). *(189)*

Charles Genfell, son of Pascoe (see 1818), continued buying local manors. This year he bought Ockwells and Kimbers, Maidenhead (see also 1852). *(581)*

Every by-street in Reading had 'a stagnant pool of putridity, the insufferable stench of a slaughter house, or the foul air of a half-choked drain'. Epidemics of typhus and occasional cases of cholera. *(126)*

From 13th century to this date the 'peculiar' jurisdiction of the Dean of Salisbury - it was normally exercised by bishops- extended over some 100 parishes. At Wokingham, where the Dean owned the tithe, he also held the rectory. Churchwardens complained that he was not fulfilling his obligations as rector. But as he, and not the Bishop, was the visitor, or ordinary, to have enforced his directions against himself would have ended his office as visitor. An appeal was made to Parliament. There is no record of the finding. *(219)*

Irish potato crop failed. Government consulted Martin Hope Sutton (see 1835). He advised the growing of quick maturing crops (turnips, beet, cabbages) and supplied the seed. *(126)*

Great Western Railway – Newbury – Hungerford line under construction. So many hundreds of navvies employed that the Vicar of Speen held special services for them. *(90)*

1847. Dr William Sewell of Exeter College founded public school in Radley Hall. He imported fine furniture and works of art for the school. The house was built in 1727. *(358)*

Huntley & Palmer moved to present site in King's Road. George Palmer designed the machinery on which the firm's success was built. It was the first continuously running machinery for making fancy biscuits, and because of it Huntley & Palmer biscuits became known throughout the

world. This year, six tons of their biscuits were seized for non-payment of the church rate. As they were Quakers, they had refused to pay. *(121)*
Great Western Railway opened to Hungerford. *(54)*
Elizabeth Barrett Browning's *Sonnets* published in Reading.
Wantage iron foundry opened, specialising in making the Berkshire Plough and a threshing machine. Later it became Wantage Engineering Co Ltd. *(163)*
The Wantage Community, founded by the Reverend William John Butler, later Dean of Lincoln, had its Convent at Belmont: two houses and girls' boarding school. Butler said to have woken up the slumbering Wantage and set it on a career of improvement and prosperity. *(168)*
Newbury County Court established. *(89)*
Berks & Hants Extension Railway (Reading-Newbury-Hungerford) opened. Cost: £20,000 a mile. *(89)*

1848. New Newbury Grammar School opened. Twenty boys elected on the full foundation of St Bartholomew's School. *(89)*
Great Western Railway locomotive 'Great Britain' pulled express of four carriages and van from Paddington to Didcot: 63¼ miles in 47 minutes. Fastest journey on record. Driver Michael Almond, fireman Richard Denman.

1849. 8 OCT. Brunel rode on first Great Western Railway train from Slough to Windsor. The South Western Railway's construction to Windsor delayed by a snapped girder on the Thames Bridge. It arrived nearly two months later (see 1846). The railways began Windsor's tourist trade. *(189)*
Duke of Sutherland bought Cliveden, Taplow. It was to burn down a second time. Both fires said to have been caused by the carelessness of a maid with a candle. New mansion was designed by Sir Charles Barry, architect of the House of Commons. *(63)*
George Street, Windsor, demolished to make way for the Western Station. It was said of it: 'There cannot be a worse street in any town in England'. *(189)*
Henry Newport MA of Pembroke College, Cambridge, became headmaster of the new Newbury Grammar School (see 1848) and another 40 boys were nominated. *(89,90)*
Reading Union Waterworks Company founded. Improvements in the town's water supply began. *(108,114,126)*
Vicarage at Compton Beauchamp built. The 'most unspoiled place in the Vale': church of white clunch and stone roof and moated manor. *(299)*
Colonel Vansittart of Cookham, a magistrate, sought formation of a Berkshire Constabulary. Six cases of arson, 30 of attempted burglary at Cookham. Few went to bed there without loaded firearms. Some put explosive balls round their properties. Another magistrate, Mr Sawyer of Bray, called a meeting of landlords and farmers who raised £180 for the establishment of a constabulary. One superintendent and six constables engaged, but effort failed through lack of money (1860-78). Sir Isaac Lyon Goldsmid, first Jew to receive the accolade, bought

Whiteknights Park, Reading. His son, Francis, first Jew to become a Queen's Counsel. Afterwards MP for Reading (1860-78).

1850. Death rate in Reading from epidemics of typhus and other diseases: 30 in every 1,000, almost double the UK death rate. *(126)*
Five railway systems now served Reading.
Caversham estate destroyed by fire, only colonnades survived (see 1718). *(291)*
Reading cattle market opened (26 November).
Old Reading Workhouse pulled down. Its oak gates survived in a garden wall in Tilehurst Road. *(230)*
National Schools in Wantage, built by public subscription, opened. Wesleyan School opened few years later and old Grammar School revived, also by public subscription. *(164)*
William Morris designed stained glass windows for Cranbourne Church. He and Burn Jones also responsible for glass in dining hall at Bradfield College (1849), where is the earliest pre-Raphaelite glass ever made. Burn Jones and Morris also did glass for All Saints', Dedworth. (see also 1780). *(291,299)*
Christopher Wordsworth, nephew of the poet, born. Became vicar of Stanford and composer of many hymns, including *Gracious Spirit, Holy Ghost. (291)*
Lord Tennyson appointed Poet Laureate. Close connection with Aldworth. Married Emily Selwood of Pipworth Manor. Tennyson called his house at Midhurst, Surrey, 'Aldworth'. Another poet, Laurence Binyon, buried at Aldworth. *(291)*

1851. Ecclesiastical parish of Bracknell formed and first parish church, Holy Trinity, built.
Population census for Windsor put population at 11,217 (see 1801).
Huntley & Palmers, Reading, now employed 200 people. Their biscuit tins (see 1840) bore trade mark of garter and buckle. Became sought after all over the world in unexpected places: Himalayan shepherds traded week's supply of milk for one tin; Lord Redesdale (1890) saw two as ornaments in Ceylonese chapel; Prince Henry of Battenberg, who died in the tropics, brought back to England in rum-filled tank made out of Huntley & Palmers tins; used as ballot boxes in Switzerland; Ugandan prayer books made to fit the 2lb tins because of white ants; Kitchener's men, after Battle of Omdurman (1898), found Sudanese sword scabbards made partly from Huntley & Palmer tins. *(120,121)*
Charles Dickens came to Reading to support a writer's society. Brought with him famous figures of the day, including Wilkie Collins, Douglas Jerrold, Mark Lemon, editor of *Punch*, and Sir John Tenniel, illustrator of *Alice in Wonderland*. They performed two plays in New Hall, London Street, blocked with carriages two hours before the curtain went up. Dickens became president of the Literary and Mechanics Institution, a Victorian education project. *(114)*

1852. Fire swept through High Street, Harwell. Nine farms, 23 cottages, livestock, hay, straw and farm produce destroyed. Fine examples of early cruck cottages escaped and are still there. *(291)*

30 JUNE. Kennet and Avon Canal sold to Great Western Railway. *(178,179)*

Charles Grenfell (see 1846) bought Taplow Court from Lord Orkney and it became the home of the Grenfell family, where the crowned heads of Europe were entertained. He later bought the manors of Lowbrooks, Cresswells, Philberts and Foxleys, all in Bray parish, making him the biggest landowner in the area. *(58)*

1853. John Wisden and John Lillywhite members of England XI which played Maidenhead cricket at Kidwells Park, Maidenhead (see 1773). *(57,58,294)*

1854. Maidenhead to High Wycombe line opened by Wycombe Railway Company (incorporated 1846), based on Maidenhead (Boyne Hill) station. Station used for only 17 years. *(242)*

1855. George Proctor, vicar of Stanford-in-the-Vale, chaplain to the Army, killed at Scutari (Crimea). *(43)*

1855. Skull of musk ox (ovibos moschatus) found at lower drift level at Taplow, Maidenhead, by the Reverend C. Kingsley and Mr John Lubbock (Lord Avebury) (see 10-8,000 BC). Now in British Museum. *(2,57)*

John Peck, first Chief Constable of Reading, succeeded by Henry Houlton. *(114,115)*

John Walters provided Finchampstead's first school buildings and planted the famous avenue of sequoia firs lining the roadside at Finchampstead Ridges. Roman Road to Silchester runs through village: known as Devil's Highway. *(291,295,296)*

William Johnson of Arborfield transported for 14 years after being convicted of larceny, following a previous conviction. It is the last record of a Berkshire man being punished in this way.

Colonel Vansittart put it to Abingdon Quarter Sessions that a county police force should be formed. In November it was suggested again, but opposed by 532 landowners and occupiers (representing half the county's acreage and more than one-third of its rateable value), led by Mr William Mount, on the ground of cost. But the County Constabulary was born on 4 December (see 1856). *(290)*

1856. Bracknell station built.

Colonel Fraser appointed first Chief Constable of Berks County Constabulary (1856-1863). He resigned to become Commissioner of the City of London Police. Lieutenant-Colonel Blandy succeeded him. Superintendent John Goldsmith took charge of the Force under Fraser. Cutlasses were carried by sergeants and constables until 1902. *(290)*

Mr Popham's horse Wild Darell won the Derby (see 1586). *(231)*

Upton Towers, Slough, built; owner, Mr Nixey, invented black paste for cleaning kitchen grates, known as black lead. *(294)*

Great Western Railway branch line to Abingdon opened. Corporation

70

had refused to allow main line (London to Oxford) to pass through the town. *(482)*

Wellington College built as national memorial to Duke of Wellington at Crowthorne. *(361,362)*

Wallingford Corn Exchange built. *(157,159,162)*

Reading's first photographic business established by Lewis family, later F.H. Dann, Broad Street.

Chief Constable's instruction: 'the expense of conveying prisoners by rail is to be avoided as much as possible. When practicable they should be conveyed by cart, and when this cannot be effected they should be marched and passed on from post to post unless there is good reason for not doing so'. Elizabethan cottage adjoining Spencers Wood Church was used as a lock-up for prisoners marched from Basingstoke to Reading. *(290)*

John Hibbert (1811-1888) of Braywick Lodge, Maidenhead, elected to Windsor Hospital Dispensary Committee. Made generous donations for hospital's extension. Later a benefactor of Maidenhead Cottage Hospital. *(211)*

1857. All Saints' School, Maidenhead, opened. *(58)*

Last scouring and cleaning of the White Horse of Uffington. These revels had sometimes been attended by 30,000 people. *(146)*

John Sutton and his brother Alfred (see 1828) now employed about 40 men and boys, and their seeds were tested to germination standards that had not existed before. *(114)*

Reading got its first plain clothes man: Dectective Constable Hernaman (see 1836,1855). *(114,115)*

Thames Conservators came into being, but there was not yet a Thames Conservancy. From 1197, City of London exercised vague authority over river (Oxford had own commissioners). *(58,270,271,275)*

County divided into six police districts. Police pay: Chief Constable - £300 pa plus travelling expenses; superintendents - £80-£100 pa; sergeant major - £65; sergeants - 23s weekly; constables - 17-21s. Police superintendents became inspectors of weights and measures. In first six months, four tons of unjust weights were confiscated. Some measures differed according to area. Corn sold by load of five quarters; wood by foot or load; statute acre for assessing rent, also a common field acre; sea coal by the ton; variety of measures other than standard bushel: in the Vale 9 gallons instead of more usual 8 to the bushel. Some magistrates vigilant in defending false weights. *(290)*

1859c. Henry Tucker's address on 'the conditions of the agricultural labourer' given at annual dinner in Faringdon. Copy in County Library. *(473)*

1859. Robert James Loyd-Lindsay of Scots Guards retired to devote himself to the Lockinge Estate, which links the villages of Lockinge and Ardington. Became Lord Wantage. The villages were planned, built and restored by Lord Wantage and his wife. Major Robert Lindsay VC carried Queen's colour at Battle of Alma (Crimea), played conspicuous part at Inkerman. Awarded VC 24 February, 1857. Equerry to Prince of Wales (Edward VII), which office was constituted for first time (1858). Pioneered voluntary movement of the Berks Corps, of which he was honorary Commandant (1860), became Brigadier General of Home Counties Brigade. Commanded Honourable Artillery Company at request of Prince of Wales (1866-81). Enthusiastic shot, originated Loyd-Lindsay Prize at Bisley. Conservative MP (1865), peer (1889). Letter to *Times* (22 July 1870) led to formation of National Society for Aid for Sick and Wounded (Franco-Prussian War), which later became the Red Cross Aid Society, of which he was chairman. As Red Cross Commissioner, present during campaign between Turkey and Serbia. Lord Lieutenant of Berks (1885) for 15 years. Succeeded Duke of Clarence as Provincial Grand Master of the Freemasons of Berkshire. Became one of the leading agriculturalists of the country, giving special attention to the breeding of shire horses and pedigree cattle; founder and chief supporter of Reading University College. His head and fine features used as model by artists (W.W. Ouless RA and Sir William Richard RA) for King Arthur and the idealised Happy Warrior portraits (see 1877). *(163,169,303)*

1860. Trades at Kingston Bagpuize (population 283) included harness maker, victualler, blacksmith, shoe and boot makers, mason, tailor, wheelwright. *(319)*

Thomas Lawrence of Bracknell awarded gold medal for invention of rubber bricks. They were used as moulds. *(502)*

1860c. Jeremiah Smith, publisher of *Faringdon Free Press,* invented and made 'the patent self-adhesive envelope'. *(43)*

Sack and hemp goods made at Wantage. Engineering just beginning there as an industry, notably at the White Horse Foundry (steam engines and farm machinery). Also Nalder's Works, agricultural engineers and founders. Henry Pulley made hats. William Liddard was auctioneer and bone merchant. *(163,164,168)*

1860. Broadmoor Criminal Lunatic Asylum being built by convict labour from Woking prison. *(290)*

High Sheriff stopped providing Javelin Men or servants in livery to keep order within the courts of assize. Duties taken over by police. *(290)*

Walter Wilder established iron foundry at Crowmarsh, which still survives. Wilder family ironmasters since late 17th century. Works spread to Reading, Henley, Wallingford and Guildford. *(162)*

1861. Beaumont Lodge, Old Windsor, became the Roman Catholic public school, Beaumont College. Henry Griffiths bought it from Warren Hastings (1789) and had Henry Emlyn FSA of Windsor, who published *Proposition for a New Order in Architecture* (1781), build present house. Emlyn designed the organ gallery in St George's Chapel, monument on Edward IV's tomb, and added choir stalls there, restoring others. New architectural order derived from local influences: Windsor Forest, Order of the Garter etc. Beaumont ranked as the third mansion in the county. *(171)*

1862c. Bracknell Market founded. Enlarged by owners (H & G Simmonds Ltd) 1920.

1862. The Reverend W. Nicholson set up famous Elephant Chapel at St Swithun's, Wickham. Eight papier mache elephants in north aisle. Brought three elephants from Paris Exhibition as examples of Fortitude, Docility and Strength. He regarded them as appropriate for angels in the church. *(291)*

Greyfriars, oldest church in Reading, reconstructed (see 1538). *(107,114)*

Mortimer Collins (1827-1867), well-known journalist, took cottage at Knowl Hill and settled there. He was once called King of the Bohemians. Wrote 23 books. *(303)*

1863. Herne's Oak blown down in Windsor Forest – or was it? The legend is of a forest keeper, perhaps Rycharde Horne, who shot and wounded a stag, became insane and ran naked through the forest (Berkshire's first streaker) with the deer's antlers tied to his head. He hanged himself on an oak. Shakespeare wrote the legend into *The Merry Wives of Windsor*. In 1796 Herne's Oak, now decayed, was cut down on George III's orders. He then chose another as the real Herne's Oak. (Edward VII was to investigate the legend. He planted new oak on original site, labelled 'Herne's Oak II'). *(171)*

Broadmoor Institution opened. Built near Caesar's Camp. Original occupants of the site called 'broom squires' or 'broom dashers'. They lived secluded life, had their own altar for worship and made brooms from the heathlands (see 1864). *(290,291)*

Abingdon Herald first published.

Maidenhead Wesleyan Schools opened. *(58)*

Parish of St Paul's, Wokingham, formed. Church built by John Walter of Bear Wood. *(219)*

Wantage Railway Passenger Station opened. *(163,483)*

At Maidenhead, 140 inhabitants sworn in as special constables to meet the fear of a French invasion. *(290)*

1864. St Sebastian's Church, Wokingham, built to meet the needs of the 'broom dashers' (see 1863), said to be an increasing population in 'a wild and remote district'. *(219)*

Watlington and Wallingford Railway authorised by Act of Parliament. Only Wallingford branch, connecting with the Great Western Railway at Cholsey, was built (Great Western Railway took it over 1871). *(162,483)*

Major move by the Huntley & Palmer partnership. They bought Bayliss' silk crepe factory, in the industrial area of Reading between the Kennet and the New Cut. Already on the site were Cannon Brewery, gas works and tobacco factory. Thomas Huntley was unhappy about the purchase (price £1,800). Site had wharf, railway close by and King's Road. At this time canals had greater range than railways. George Palmer saw the site, equipped with new machinery, growing fast. He was right. Eventually the railway laid sidings into the factory to collect the biscuits. This was the beginning of Huntley & Palmer's tremendous impact upon the enonomic and civic life of Reading. *(120,121)*

1865. Aldermaston village lock-up used for last time: for a drunk. It is still on the recreation ground. *(501)*

1866. Thames Conservancy came into being through Act of Parliament. *(270,271,275)*

Mr John Walter built St Paul's School, Wokingham. *(219)*

12 JULY. Until this date the minister of Wokingham (Wokingham was a chapelry of Sonning) was called a perpetual curate. Under the District Church Tithes Act (1865), the Ecclesiastical Commissioners made the parish a rectory and the incumbent a rector. The new parish of St Paul's became a rectory on 2 August. Sandhurst, Arborfield and Bear Wood also became rectories. *(219)*

1867. Maidenhead Roman Catholics began separate meetings. *(58)*

Walter James Blackett, who sold books in Northbrook Street, Newbury, was joined by Thomas Wheildon Turner and they began producing the *Newbury Weekly News. (90)*

Wantage Town Lands Trust built new almshouses (1867-1871). Tenants received up to £250 pa. *(163)*

Windsor and Eton Cricket Club formed. *(189)*

Assize court moved from Abingdon to Reading, but Abingdon retained court of quarter sessions, which was first granted in 1609. *(38)*

1868. Compulsory church rates abolished in Reading. Previously, nonconformists had to pay taxes to a church in which they did not believe. *(101,126)*

East Hagbourne villages picked 10,013 bushels of hops. The hop gardens were centred on Manor Farm. *(43)*

Residents of Grove threatened to take Wantage Council to law for polluting Letcombe brook with sewage and refuse. Wantage and Letcombe were similarly accused by Grove again in 1877-8. *(43)*

1869. 28 JULY. *Maidenhead Advertiser* began publication. Started by Edward Bushell Prosser. Town population approximately 5,000. Nothing is known of Mr Prosser. *(58)*

Maidenhead Football Club formed. It was one of the original entrants in the FA Cup. (Defeated by Tottenham Hotspurs in divisional semi-final.) *(58)*

Aldermaston Co-operative Industrial and Provident Society Ltd formed. Eventually bought out by Basingstoke Co-operative Society. *(501)*

First bicycle race in Berks. H.J. Timberlake of Maidenhead, on a velocipede, challenged Louis Rumball, winner of the Chertsey Steeplechase, to a race over 1 mile on Maidenhead Thicket for £10 a side and silver tankard. The cyclist came to grief in an accident said to have been caused by gypsies. Rumball finished the mile in 4 minutes 57 seconds. Great crowd watched.

Dr Christopher Wordsworth, well-known hymn writer, vicar of Goosey (1850-69), became resident canon of Westminster; afterwards Bishop of Lincoln. *(43)*

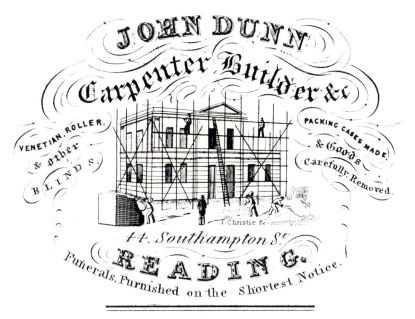

J. DUNN respectfully acknowledges the very liberal encouragement he has received for the last 16 years, and begs to assure those who may honor him with a continuance that no effort shall be spared on his part to secure their approbation.

MANUFACTURER OF SURGICAL APPARATUS TO THE ROYAL BERKSHIRE HOSPITAL.

J. D. has the honor to announce that he supplies Surgeons with every kind of Apparatus for the treatment of Fractures and Distortions of the Limbs. constructed eithe·   ` the most moder·

~nts, or ′   ᵃv be r·

County welfare through private enterprise, 1843.

xxi

Hone's General Coach Office
KING-STREET READING.
(Adjoining the George Inn.)

Reduced Fares to LONDON
BY THE
OMNIBUS.
Inside 8s. Outside 5s.
Mornings at 10 o'Clock.

TO LONDON
THE TELEGRAPH FAST COACH,
Through MAIDENHEAD and SLOUGH; every day at Twelve (except Sunday,) to *Nelson's* Black Bear, Piccadilly, and Blossom's Inn, Lawrence Lane, Cheapside; from whence it returns every Morning at 11; and Black Bear, Piccadilly at a quarter before 12.

———oOo———

"STAR" Coach to BATH and BRISTOL,
Through MARLBOROUGH, DEVIZES, and MELKSHAM, every Morning (except Sunday) at a quarter before Nine o'Clock to the York House Bath, and White Lion, BRISTOL.

TO LONDON.--The ZEPHYR, through WINDSOR,
Every day at half past One.

———oOo———

COACHES DAILY TO

Oxford	Brighton	Marlow	Portsmouth	Windsor
Wallingford	Guildford	Bath	Basingstoke	Wantage
Maidenhead	Petersfield	Bristol	Newbury	Faringdon
Winchester	Odiham	Horsham	Marlborough	Cirencester
Alton	Horndean	Southampton	Monmouth	Gloucester &
Farnham	Wycombe	Gosport	Hereford	Worthing.

Wm. HONE & Co. Proprietors.

	£	s.	d.
PAID OUT......			
CARRIAGE......			
BOOKING ...			
PORTERAGE...			

SOCIABLES to Streatley, Newbury, Basingstoke, Windsor, Wallingford, Henley and Maidenhead, daily

White, Printer & Binder, Reading.

The way to Metropolis, early 1800's. (BRO)

1870. Wesleyans began meeting in St Leonard's Square chapel, Wallingford, where they still are. *(162)*

Bracknell Cattle and Poultry Market established. One of largest egg markets in Southern England. Became centre for distribution to government slaughterhouses. Originally horse and hiring fair, when cooks carried basting spoons and housemaids a broom. *(502)*

Abingdon Grammar School moved to present site (see 1563). *(38)*

Hungerford Town Hall and Corn Exchange erected at a cost of about £4,000. *(54)*

Cliveden, Taplow, bought by the Duke of Westminster. *(63)*

Six Thames steamers running between Oxford and Kingston. First, the 'Alaska', was built at Bourne End by the Maidenhead firm of Horsham. (Three, 'Kingston', 'Windsor' and 'Cliveden', were shipped abroad in World War I. 'Cliveden' was sunk in Mediterranean.) *(58)*

William Lassall of Ray Lodge, Maidenhead, became president of the Royal Astronomical Society. *(58)*

Peat digging a local industry at Newbury. *(89)*

Pedlar's Act revealed that there were 1,139 pedlars in the county, one for every 110 inhabitants. Vagrancy a problem due to poor economic conditions. The following numbers of tramps were relieved: Abingdon 1,293; Bradfield 1,043; Cookham 3,304; Easthampstead 1,734; Faringdon 1,367; Hungerford 1,328; Newbury 2,819; Reading 5,527; Wallingford 2,968; Wantage 652; Windsor 3,974; Wokingham 474. *(290)*

1871. Maori chief George King Hispango from Wanganui, New Zealand, died at Letcombe Regis. Buried at St Andrew's. *(43)*

Maidenhead Roman Catholic School opened. *(58)*

Present Maidenhead station opened. *(242)*

New buildings for Reading School, in 13 acres South of London Road near Royal Berks Hospital, opened by Prince of Wales, who drove over from Windsor. He got some dirt in his eye, which was removed at the hospital before the ceremony. *(114)*

1872. Sir Gilbert East of Hall Place, Maidenhead, summoned for using steam locomotive on highway when not preceded by a man carrying a red flag. Sir Gilbert gave orders to his lodge keeper that any policeman appearing was to be turned off the premises, and if he refused to go, to be 'kicked off'. After the case, Sir Gilbert accused the officer of committing perjury. During police investigations, Lady Wilsher hailed the Chief Constable with her parasol when walking on Maidenhead Thicket, saying that she had 'heard in society' that he had been abused by Sir Gilbert in front of the justices 'most undeservedly'. *(290)*

Newbury stocks used for the last time for Mark Tuck. He had disturbed a church service with a drunken brawl. Stocks now in Newbury Museum. *(90)*

Frederick George Baylis, aged 31, became partner in *Maidenhead Advertiser*. He bought out the syndicate the following year and founded the firm which still runs today. *(58)*

1873. Mr W.W. Aston (his family owned New York) bought Cliveden from the Duke of Westminster and emigrated to England. *(58)*

1874. Wantage tram service opened. Horses hauled first trams. *(165, 166,455).*

1875. The Maidenhead Waterworks Act, covering also Cookham and Bray. Pumping station in College Avenue, reservoir Castle Hill. Existing local company was bought out for £225. Attempt by Maidenhead Corporation to set up undertaking foiled. Opposition from Great Western Railway Company. *(489)*

Warren Hastings returned from India (13 June). Two days later had reunion with his wife at Maidenhead, probably at Orkney Arms (later Skindles). He asked her to meet him on Maidenhead Bridge. *(57)*

Wokingham choirman James Wynn died aged 83. Remembered pre-organ days, when singing was accompanied by clarinet, bassoon and bass viol (church accounts show item: violincello £5 5s 0d). *(219)*

1876. Maidenhead Waterworks company board resolved that cheque for £500 be drawn in favour of contractor, but not paid until the funds were in the bank. Three directors loaned £1,000. *(489)*

Remains of Roman villa excavated at East Challow. *(291)*

Inspector Joseph Drewett (Hungerford) and PC Thomas Shorter (Shefford) murdered by poachers near Folly Cross Roads. *(290)*

Wantage (see 1874) ran England's first steam tram. *(165-166)*

Newbury District Water Company established. *(89,90)*

1877. Maidenhead people began collecting a fund to start a cottage hospital for a population of about 7,000. *(58)*

Watlington House, Reading, became Kendrick Girls' School, founded by Reading Corporation, a pioneer in municipal schools. Built by Sir Christopher Wren (1688) for Samuel Watlington (mayor 1695 and 1710), who tried to revive cloth trade. His wife Anne was famous botanist and apothecary. *(230)*

14 JULY. Prince of Wales unveiled statue of King Alfred, sculpted by Count Glichen, at Wantage. It was gift of Colonel Loyd-Lindsay VC (see 1859) who had modelled for the head. *(157)*

Warwicks opened in Reading, making bicycles. They exported to Dayton, Ohio, USA, to the Wright Brothers, aeronautical pioneers (they made first controlled flight, 1903). Warwicks later made the stop-me-and-buy-one ice cream tricycles for Walls. *(114)*

Walter Biggs' School re-founded as Wallingford School (see 1659). Buildings now part of Wallingford Upper School. *(162)*

Didcot to Newbury line opened by Great Western Railway. *(484)*

1878. Wantage new Town Hall opened. Wantage Water Company extended its mains, putting an end to threatened legal action by residents of Grove (see 1868). *(163)*

Swan marking, during the annual Swan-upping Ceremony on Thames, changed to making nicks on the birds' beaks. Swan a royal bird; ceremony of marking the swans centuries old. Dyers and Vintners companies, who had the right from time immemorial of owning and marking swans, and the Queen's Swan Master (currently Mr John Turk of Cookham) take part in annual Upping Ceremony in July. *(270)*

1879. Maidenhead Cottage Hospital opened. First case a 14-year-old paper sorter with a scalded leg 22 November. He remained there for 11 weeks. Previously Windsor Infirmary and Reading Hospital had taken Maidenhead patients. Mr John Hibbert of Braywick gave £100; Mr W. Woodbridge, local builder, had tendered £1,700. The town showered gifts on the hospital of beds, sheets, blankets, furniture, china and shrubs for the garden. *(503)*

First sod of the Didcot, Newbury and Southampton Railway turned.

1880. Abingdon's last MP elected. Borough constituency merged with county in 1885. *(38)*

William and Ernest Renshaw, twins of Waltham St Lawrence, began remarkable career at tennis. Were to win every major doubles and singles event open to them for ten years, to become the creators of modern lawn tennis. *(294)*

1881. Boy frozen to death in blizzard on Berkshire Downs. *(291)*

Heraldic glass removed from St Nicholas' Church, Abingdon, and transferred to County Hall. It had been made by J.H. Russell of Oxford (1829-30). The arms are of families connected with the neighbourhood. *(42)*

H. Dodd, originator of Thames Barge Race, died. Tomb depicting race at Farnham Royal, Slough. Sailing barge fleet numbered about 3,000. *(270)*

Wallingford Congregationalists disbanded (see 1799). Their church was later taken over by the Roman Catholics. *(162)*

Maidenhead a centre for bicycle manufacture: Timberlakes and Pilot Cycle Company. *(57)*

1883. Shop workers in Maidenhead appealed for early closing one night a week at 5pm in these terms: 'we are close to a magnificent river with every facility for enjoyment thereon, besides numerous other sports which would invigorate the soul and raise in the mind sublime ideas . . . summer is now rapidly approaching with all her beauties and we are compelled to stay at business until 8 o'clock . . . we don't ask for all the year round, say from May to September'. (First early closing was on four nights at 7 pm.)

Many injured in clash at Maidenhead when Salvationist woman, Major Brown, led Blue Ribbon Army headed by band in temperance demonstration against 'the demon drink' down High Street to Chapel Arches. Here they met, head on, a bibulous brigade: the self-styled Yellow Ribbon Army. *(58)*

Mrs Simkin's pinks first went on sale at Turner's Nursery, Slough. They were raised by Mr Simkin, workhouse master at both Slough and Maidenhead, and named after his wife. *(428)*

Reading Central Library and Museum opened. *(126)*

Maidenhead water works engineer had his wages increased to 30s a week (from 26s) for the summer months only 'for increased pumping due to the roads being watered'. Dusty roads were a constant source of complaint. *(498)*

Percy Smith of Letcombe Bassett bequeathed £5,000 to establish Wantage Cottage Hospital. His sister, Mrs Harriet Firth of Wantage, bequeathed £2,000 for setting up the Firth Medical Dispensary for the Poor and Deserving of Wantage and Letcombe Bassett. *(163)*

Act of Parliament passed for regulating steam launches on the Thames. *(270)*

1885. Wokingham got its first mayor when the title of Chief Magistrate of Wokingham changed from 'The Alderman of Wokingham' to 'The Mayor'. *(219)*

South Berks constituency represented by W.G. Mount of Wasing Place (Conservative). From 1885 until present (except 1903 and 1923 Liberal) Newbury seat held by Conservatives; 1885-1922 by Sir William Mount. *(90)*

Sir Gilbert Clayton East of Hall Place, Hurley, told Select Committee on Thames Rights of Way that there was no such thing as a public landing place in the Upper Thames. The public believed that the Thames Conservators, of whom Sir Gilbert was one, were not acting in the public's interest as they were expected to do, but in the interest of riparian owners. *(58,275)*

Newbury District Hospital opened, one of the first cottage hospitals in the country. Cottage hospitals were cheaper to run than general hospitals, bed for bed. *(89)*

28 JULY. Newbury's new Grammar School in Enborne Road opened. *(89,90)*

George Henry Vansittart died. Succeeded at Bisham Abbey by Edward Vansittart-Neale, son of former rector of Taplow (see 1769). Helped promote annual conference of Co-operators, became general secretary of the Co-operative Union (1873-1891), prominent in International Co-operative Alliance. *(78)*

1886. Roman villa discovered on Castle Hill, Maidenhead, by Mr Richard Silver. Coins of Tetricus (AD 267-273), pieces of Samian Ware etc unearthed during building operations. Currently crated in Maidenhead Town Hall vaults. *(57,58)*

Price of racing boats: eights £60; fours £35; pairs £22; scullers' boats £15; pair-oared gig or skiff £23 (mahogany £25). *(270)*

Woolley Hall, Maidenhead, home of George Dunn, expert on astronomy, arboriculture, horology and old books. *(291)*

Riverside hotels advertised cups, cocktails and grogs for Thames water picnics. *(270.*

Great Western railway guide announced: 'horses and carriages are conveyed to or from Windsor, Taplow, Maidenhead, Bourne End, Great Marlow, Henley, Reading, Pangbourne, Goring, Wallingford, Abingdon and Oxford, and horses only to and from Cookham. Previous intimation should be given to the station master. *(244)*

ABOVE: Reading s age of steam.

BELOW: The Thames at Newbury.

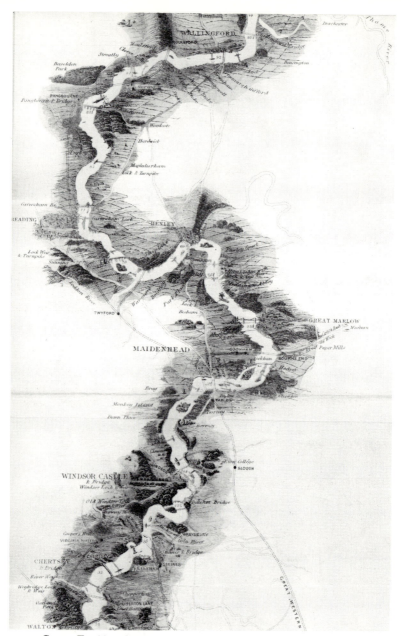

George Tombleson's 'panoramic' view of the Berkshire Thames, c.1894.

xxiv

1888. Local Government Act established county councils. Rural government until now had been in the hands of magistrates meeting at quarter sessions.

1889. Reading police constables earned £1 3s 4d weekly; sergeants £1 13s 3d (after 8 years' service); inspectors £100-115 annually. Life pension scheme and 7 days' annual leave with pay (see 1836, 1855, 1857). *(115)*

D.H. Brown, nurseryman of Maidenhead, exhibited dahlias at Crystal Palace show. His wife and son John made Maidenhead-raised dahlias world famous.(John Brown currently National Dahlia Society president and Chelsea Show judge). *(58)*

Berkshire County Council came into existence. The new councils were the first elected bodies for the rural areas, but had some authority over borough matters, although the boroughs, of which Wallingford (1155) is the oldest, enjoyed considerable autonomy. Reading became a county borough, giving it the powers of both borough and county councils. First chairman of Berks County Council was Mr W.G. Mount, MP for South Berks, of Wasing Place. He served for 16 years. *(499)*

1890. Forth Railway Bridge opened. Designed by Sir Benjamin Baker of Bowden Green, Pangbourne. Baker and John Fowler constructed London's Metropolitian Railway. Baker was consulting engineer for the Aswan Dam and designed the vessel which carried Cleopatra's Needle to London. *(303)*

Maidenhead Workhouse receiving 1,000 tramps a year. Arnold Thompson wrote to the Maidenhead Advertiser: 'The nuisance and cost is the monster scandal of the day'. *(58)*

1891. 17 JULY. The Prince of Wales, Duke of Edinburgh and the Duke of Clarence and Avondale waited on the lawn of the riverside George Inn, Bray (now called The Waterside), for the Kaiser. Tegg's launches decorated with marguerites, were moored nearby. They were all going upstream to Henley Royal Regatta. The Kaiser sent a messenger from Windsor to say that he had a cold and could not come. *(58)*

One out of every 19 of Maidenhead's population appeared before the magistrates. The tramp population rose to 12,593. There were 8,395 people in common lodging houses and 43,350 boats brought 256,560 passengers into Maidenhead. *(290)*

Palmer Park, in which is statue of philanthropist George Palmer, opened. He and Martin John Sutton made freemen of the borough.

1892. University Extension Delegacy founded University Extension College, part housed in hospitium of the abbey, part in old vicarage of St Laurence's Church. The old vicarage had been bought by Herbert Sutton, who was chairman of the council of the School of Science and Art. First principal Halford Mackinder. W.M. Childs one of first lecturers. It had grown from earliest branch of university extension movement in Oxford and was first (other than Oxford and Cambridge) to have residential system. Farmers' families flocked to new university and its chief study became agriculture (see 1355, 1827, 1903). *(133-136)*

Last broad gauge train, the 'Cornishman' from London to Penzance, ran down the Great Western Railway main line across the county. Conversion to narrow gauge completed on main line in approximately 24 hours. *(242-243)*

1893. The Reverend W.G. Sawyer, rector of Taplow, declared: 'Much of the degeneracy of modern youth arises from the demoralising influence of football which is a rowdy and gambling game. Saturday matches cause neglect of religious duties on Sunday'.

1 MAY. Didcot, Newbury and Southampton Junction Railway opened for business. *(484)*

Correspondent wrote to *Maidenhead Advertiser:* 'I am surprised that the *Advertiser* is to accept subscriptions for the wives and children of miners who will not work'.

Department of Agriculture established at Reading University, teaching the principles of agriculture to teachers of rural schools: a continuation of Saturday morning classes begun the previous year. *(133-136)*

Reading Corporation Fire Brigade formed.

Royal Tapestry manufactory established at Windsor.

1894. Chairman of Maidenhead Waterworks Company met Borough Surveyor to discuss 'the high consumption of water in the Park Street public urinal'. *(498)*

Maidenhead Borough Council agreed not to adopt the Public Libraries Act. There had been much controversy over the establishment of a free library. Opponents believed that the well off could afford to use circulating libraries and that the poor could get their reading from working men's clubs. Free libraries would provide accommodation for idlers and loafers (there was much unemployment). Suggested that council provide seats round the market place where the 'loafers' would 'enjoy themselves far better than in a library'. *(490)*

The British Dairying Institute moved from Aylesbury to Reading University, eventually to occupy a new wing of the college on the corner of Valpy Street.

Maidenhead Commercial School Company Ltd built town's first secondary school, called the Modern School. It became Grammar School and later Desborough School. *(58)*

J.D.M. Pearce, twice mayor of Maidenhead, in address to Anti-Smoking League, said: 'smokers have dark muddy complexions, which are often transferred to their children, who are thus cheated out of being good looking'.

Record flood levels in Thames Valley.

Berkshire Police Bicycle Corps formed. It was claimed that reliable information could be more readily circulated to constables in this way than by telegram. First pilot run to test the theory was from Maidenhead to Wallingford (29 miles, 8 police stations. Time: 3 hours 15 minutes). Second run from Sandhurst to Newbury (30 miles, 8 police stations. Time: 3 hours 12 minutes). *(290)*

Nurses' training scheme began at Windsor Hospital. *(211)*

Local Government Act set up urban and rural district councils and parish councils in villages, with limited powers, completing a new pattern of local government for rural areas. Urban district councils came into being for towns which did not have borough status. Slough became a civil parish this year, and was governed by an urban district council until it received its charter of incorporation as a borough 1938-39.

1895. George Herring built the Haven of Rest almshouses at Maidenhead. *(58)*

The Hon Evelyn Ellis of Datchet made his first drive, in a 4 hp Panhard-Levassor with a Daimler engine, to Windsor. His average speed over 56 miles was 9.84 mph. It was the first privately owned motor car in England. Whole villages turned out to see this remarkable horseless carriage when it toured the Berkshire lanes.*(294)*

1896. Mrs Annie Dyer of 45 Kensington Road, Reading, hanged. Her crime was known as the Baby Farm Case. *(114)*

Reading University became examination centre for National Diploma in Dairying.

1897. Buscot model village built. *(299)*

Science building added to Wantage Grammar School. *(164)*

Reading Police Station got a telephone, but for the use of the Chief Constable only. *(115)*

1898. Lambourne Valley Railway opened. *(480)*

Legal battle to free Windsor Bridge of tolls led by Joseph Taylor through the Queen's Bench, High Court of Appeal and House of Lords (see 1903). *(342)*

1899. Alfred Harmsworth, later Lord Northcliffe, the Press Lord who lived at Calcot Park, bought his first motor car. His motoring friends brought their vehicles to Calcot at the weekends. *(294)*

Colonel Sir Charles Gervaise Boxall of Battlemead, Maidenhead, invented and organised the City of London Imperial Volunteers (the CIVs) for service in the South African War. *(58)*

Twentieth Century

Agricultural Berkshire disappeared in the twentieth century. The county moved from the fields into the age of technology. The internal combustion engine replaced steam and brought the first air mail to Windsor. Domestic use of electricity, which spread partly with the help of a Maidenhead inventor, was a prelude to the electronics industry. The discoveries of William Herschel of Windsor and Slough led to space satellites and Winkfield's satellite tracking station. British scientists at Harwell led the world into the Atomic Age. The county's great estates became centres of research and the descendents of the agricultural workers staffed the offices that administered the technology.

The aftermath of World War II brought a people problem. Massive housing shortages, coupled with one of the highest population growth rates in the country, led to towns being largely rebuilt and rural acres eaten up with housing estates. Farming mechanised beyond the wildest dreams of Jethro Tull. Fertilizers were delivered from the factory.

Berkshire became linked with the North Atlantic Treaty Organisation through its air bases, and British nationals from the Near and Far East gave a multi-racial look to some of its towns.

But the new royal house was the House of Windsor, and in 1974 the Queen made her historic river journey through the new Royal Borough of Windsor and Maidenhead, to mark the reorganisation of local government. On 1 April this reorganisation gave away the ancient heart of Berkshire – the Vale of the White Horse – to Oxfordshire, and in this readjustment of county boundaries, Slough, Bucks, became Slough, Berks. The Queen's journey was from Hurley to Magna Carta Island, reminiscent of 1215 and 1688, when the course of English history had twice before been set on a different course.

1900. Lord Wantage bought the Victoria Cross pictures by Chevalier Desanges and presented them to Wantage. Hung in old Corn Exchange, which was renamed Victoria Cross Gallery. *(163)*

Alfred Harmsworth of Calcott (see 1899) sponsored round Britain car rally, for which 83 vehicles entered. *(294)*

1901. James Herbert Benyon, Lord Lieutenant of Berks, son of John Fellowes, assumed name of Benyon on death of his uncle, when he succeeded to Englefield.

Huntley & Palmer, now employing 6,000, won two Grand Prizes at Paris Exhibition. *(120,121)*

Hungerford population fell from 2,696 (1851) to 2,364 (1901).

King Alfred's Grammar School (now King Alfred's School) rebuilt in Portway, Wantage. *(164,168)*.

Bronze Age barrows at Sunningdale excavated. Fragments of urns in Reading Museum. *(291)*

1902. 9 DEC. Major J.E. Pearce switched on Maidenhead's first electric power station. He built Galway Power Station and invented many devices in common use in power stations in the UK. He also built Maidenhead's first concrete houses. When the power was switched on 'there were 28 services ready for the new illuminant', the *Maidenhead Advertiser* reported, 'which probably represented nearly 500 lights. Mrs Brown-Potter of the Fishery Estate had her switches open and was probably one of the first to receive the light'. *(58)*

James Benyon (see 1901), president of the Court of Governors of Reading University College, became first chancellor and Dr Childs first vice-chancellor. This year, the university added horticulture to its curriculum. *(114)*

Thomas Kelly, landlord of the Bramshill Hunt Inn, Arborfield, severely reprimanded by the justices for refusing to find shelter and refreshment for two men and two horses travelling from Newbury to Woking, Surrey.

Inspector Charles Goddard of Berkshire Constabulary, who brought the complaint, reported 'the law being too expensive the injured party did not indict Kelly, this being the only course at present open'. *(290)*

Of the 667 public houses in the county, 256 exhibited a notice 'all spirits sold here are diluted'. Wokingham had 15 fully licensed and 15 beer houses, or one for every 94 inhabitants. Magistrates felt that it was too well provided. *(290)*

Prospect Park, Reading, opened. *(114)*

Berkshire Police issued with first orders for dealing with the motor car. Those travelling at more than 15-16 miles an hour to be stopped for speeding. *(290)*

1903. 24 JAN. *Wokingham & Bracknell Gazette (and County Review)* appeared. Founded by Francis Staniland. Became *Wokingham and Bracknell Times* 1951.

Maidenhead Bridge freed of tolls by Joseph Taylor's campaign (see 1898). *(342)*

Edward Sharwood Smith appointed head of St Bartholomew's Grammar School, Newbury. *(89,90)*

The Reverend F.T. Wethered published *St Mary's Hurley in the Middle Ages*, containing his translations from the original Latin of the early deeds of Hurley's Benedictine Priory. *(84)*

1904. Wokingham Market revived by Thimbleby & Shoreland of Reading.

Association for the Advancement of the Higher Education of the Working Classes in Reading formed. This was the beginning of the Workers' Education Association (WEA). Dr Albert Mansbridge, founder of the WEA said it was epoch-making and set the pattern for branches in England and overseas. It was brought about by four elements: the Co-operative Movement (Reading's was particularly enlightened), adult schools, trade unions, and Reading University College, whose principal, W.M. Childs, played a leading part and devised the first constitution for a WEA branch, later adopted throughout UK and dominions. *(124)*

William Childs MA became Principal of Reading University (see 1892, 1905). *(133-136)* Electric trams introduced to Reading. *(114,133)*

1904. Albert Heybourne imported 1904 de Dion Boutonville car, said to be the first car to be owned by Maidonian. Locals set up Anti-Dangerous Motorists' League. *(58)*

Reading Police clerks provided with their first typewriter. *(114,115)*

Reading University given new site by Alfred Palmer (see 1905). *(133-136)*

Maidenhead High School for Girls opened. (Now Newlands School.)

Marks & Spencer opened Penny Bazaar in West Street, Reading. *(114)*

Rufus Isaacs, MP for Reading (1904-13), lived at Foxhall. *(114)*

Lady Rose of Hardwick House brought two gondolas and a gondolier back from Venice. She used them for shopping trips to Reading, transferring to her carriage at Caversham Bridge. *(114)*

Winston Churchill flung into Thames at a week-end party given by Mr and Mrs W.H. Grenfell at Taplow Court, Maidenhead. Lady Desborough wrote in memoirs: 'he swam composedly'. He went in again during a water fight five years later. Taplow Court parties attracted only the best people. *(58)*

1905. Moving pictures first shown at Maidenhead at Mr George Gude's Pavilion. *(58)*

W.H. Grenfell became Baron Desborough. *(58)*

King Edward and Queen Alexandra cruised to Monkey Island, Bray, where they had tea, from the king's boathouse, Datchet. *(58)*

Mortimer celebrated as collecting ground for butterflies and moths. Species to have been found there in abundance: Purple Emperor, White Admiral, Wood White, Tortoishell, Duke of Burgundy, Silver Washed Fritillary, Holly Blue, Death's Head Hawk, Convolvulus Hawk. *(226)*

Newbury Racecourse opened. Previously, racing took place on the Wash and later Enborne Heath. Course built by Mr L.H. Baxendale and Mr Porter. *(91)*

Twenty-four coins of the reign of Allectus (AD 193) found in Shrivenham well. *(291)*

Workers' Educational Association adopted as new title for Association for the Advancement of the Higher Education of the Working Classes in Reading. Annual subscription 7d, payable at the rate of 1d a week. *(114,123,124)*

7 JUNE. Foundation stone for Reading University extension laid. George William Palmer and Alfred Palmer (see 1904) jointly with Lady Wantage contributed more than £200,000 in addition to property and land to endow university. Alfred gave six acres adjoining Royal Berkshire Hospital and endowment of £50,000 for new buildings. *(136)*

1906. Viscount Astor, who had bought Cliveden, Taplow, gave it to his son as a wedding present this year when he married Nancy Langhorne of Virginia. The second Viscount set up the famous Cliveden Stud. *(63)*

Reading Police first began to use photography. *(113,114)*

1907. King Edward VII Hospital, Windsor, built. *(171,211)*

Dr William Gordon Stables (see 1840) founded Caravan Club. Had huge horse-drawn caravan, now in Bristol Museum. *(291)*

1908. Maidenhead Borough rate fell by 6d in the £ to 3s 6d. *(58)*

Olympic Games organised by Lord Desborough of Taplow Court, an outstanding athlete. He swam across Niagara Falls Pool twice, stroked an eight across the Channel, climbed Matterhorn by three different routes, fenced for England, was Thames Punting Champion, president of the MCC and Lawn Tennis Association, an Oxford three-miler, a war correspondent, author, and as MP largely responsible for the Port of London Act and the revision of police pay. *(58)*

Kenneth Grahame (1859-1932) published *Wind in the Willows*. He lived at Church Cottage, Pangbourne, and at Cookham. Other books: *The Golden Age* (1895) and *Dream Days* (1898). *(292,370)*

1908. Edward VII laid foundation stone of new Windsor Hospital. It had an accident and emergency ward on ground floor and a horse ambulance to bring in casualties. Out-patients casualties in first year amounted to 6,105. *(211)*

1909. A.E. Preston, historian and benefactor of Abingdon, elected mayor without being a member of the council. *(35,38)*

Newbury old Town Hall, with Shambles below where butter, cheese, poultry and meat were sold, demolished. *(90)*

Newbury County Girls' School opened. *(91)*

1910. George V shed name of Saxe-Coburg and began House of Windsor. *(189)*

The Two Bobs – Alden and Adams – topped bill at the London Tivoli. They introduced ragtime to London. Both lived at Maidenhead. (Alden died 1932, Adams 1948). *(58)*

Arthur Grice, J. Talford Wood and C.M. Keiller began building a new light car, the GWK, at Cordwallis Works, Maidenhead. Thus began Maidenhead's brief experience as a centre of motor engineering. *(58,318)*

Maidenhead's first cinema opened: The Picture Theatre, Bridge Road. The main attraction was a film of Maidenhead High Street on a wet and dull day. Mr Boyle Lawrence and Mr Frederick Mouillot launched the enterprise. *(58)*

First Girl Guide Troop, Miss Baden-Powell's Own, formed at Pinkneys Green, Maidenhead. *(219)*

1911. Head of firm of Dickinson guest of Major Morrison at Basildon, who suggested the name 'Basildon Bond' for firm's well-known writing paper. *(291)*

Shire Hall, Reading, opened by Sir Robert Mowbray, to house the new County Council. *(499)*

First aerial post service from London to Windsor. Tom Sopwith flew over Windsor Castle and landed on Royal Golf Links at the east end of the Castle. The King and the young princes, George, Henry and John were there to greet him when he landed. *(489)*

Foundation stone of Royal Berks Hospital extension laid with full ₘasonic honours by Lord Ampthill, Pro Grand Master of England of the Ancient Fraternity of Freemasons.

Last meeting of the Royal Buckhounds at Maidenhead. They had the longest surviving link of any local hunt with the mediaeval sporting kings. *(58,402)*

The Marquis of Downshire, who was captain of Wokingham Fire Brigade, gave an ox for the George V coronation celebrations.

Second Police Reserve (Special Constables) set up. It was organised by Colonel Ricardo of Cookham. Special Constable, the Marquis of Downshire of Easthampstead Park, provided Superintendent Goddard with a motor car and acted as his chauffeur. The numbers were: towns: Abingdon 47, Newbury 80, Wallingford 26, Wokingham 29, Maidenhead 62. County districts: Abingdon 136, Faringdon 78,

Maidenhead 172, Newbury 148, Reading 173, Wantage 89, Windsor 113, Wokingham 274. *(290)*

1912. Research Institute in Dairying set up at Reading University. *(114,133-136)*

Present Boulters Lock, Maidenhead, built (see 1746, 1829). It is the largest lock on the Thames. *(58,271,272)*

Titanic disaster. Mrs Carter, niece of the Hughes brothers (Reverend John Hughes, vicar of Longcot, and his brother, author of *Tom Brown's Schooldays*) and her husband, the Reverend Carter, drowned. *(291)*

Isaac Early of East Garston died aged 104. *(291)*

1913. Reading one of four towns chosen for Bowley's 1913 investigation into poverty. It found 40 per cent of the children of Reading had insufficient food and clothing to keep them in good health.

Maidenhead suspended third delivery of post on Thursdays and collection from certain boxes between 4.15 and 5 pm 'in order that a half-holiday may be given to as many postmen as possible'.

1914. World War I began and brought heavy casualties to Berkshire regiments. Began with loss of nine officers and 414 men of the 1st Battalion. *(287,288)*

Evacuees from Belgium billeted in Maidenhead. *(58)*

Taplow Court, home of Lord Desborough, became rest centre for nurses. Maidenhead Hospital cleared of civilian patients to make way for war wounded. Viscount Astor built Cliveden Hospital in his grounds and gave it to the Canadian Army. It was supervised by Lady Nancy Astor; 23,000 men were to pass through it. *(58)*

Soup kitchens opened in Maidenhead. Food shortages. Ex-Prime Minister H.H. Asquith refused second slice of bread at Skindles, Maidenhead's top class dining-out spot. *(58)*

Prisoner-of-war camp for German officers set up at Holyport. *(58)*

Bombed-out London Jews set up community at Maidenhead. *(58)*

Bisham Abbey turned into hospital for Belgian soldiers. *(78)*

More than 100 men from Aldermaston joined the forces. This was the highest average per head of population for any town or village in the UK. *(501)*

Reading University students enlisted. Royal Flying Corps and trainee munitions workers occupied university buildings. *(114,144)*

Suffragettes set fire to St Mary's Church, Wargrave, and destroyed building except for Norman tower (see 1916). Mrs Una Duval of Sunningwell, friend of Mrs Pankhurst, chained herself to Buckingham Palace railings and went on hunger strike in prison. *(291)*

At Poperinghe, Belgium, British HQ Flanders, was built a second Skindles Hotel. The original, at Maidenhead, adjoined the Brigade of Guards Boat Club. Also at Poperinghe, the Toc H Movement was formed. *(291)*

Major Edward Norkett of Maidenhead built dam, with aid of unemployed, to stem flood waters of the Thames. It was 1,000ft long and cost £300. Regarded with suspicion by Thames Conservancy and some property owners, for fear that it would alter the course of flood waters. *(58)*

Wilts and Berks Canal abandoned (see 1810). *(273,274)*

Rufus Isaacs (see 1904) created Lord Reading of Erleigh. He became Ambassador to USA, Lord Chief Justice and Viceroy of India. *(122)*

Newbury Racecourse became prisoner-of-war camp. *(90,91)*

1915. 2 JAN. Norkett's Dam (see 1914) burst. Maidenhead inundated. *(58)*

Thornton Smith began rebuilding Shoppenhangers Manor, Maidenhead, in the style of a 17th century merchant's home using material of correct date. He filled it with treasures. Thornton Smith was one of the greatest authorities on the design and character of furniture in Europe since the Renaissance. He and his brother Ernest ran one of London's top antique furnishing and decorating firms.

Cookham Rural District Council appointed an 'early riser and total abstainer' to the position of temporary surveyor. He gave the following undertaking: 'I will try not to introduce any new ideas'.

Engineering department of Huntley & Palmer, Reading, made shell cases as subcontractors of the Pulsometer Co. Huntley & Palmer's railway system used as marshalling yard for munitions made in Reading. *(120,121)*

1916. 1 JULY. War casualties in Royal Berkshires still mounting: 2nd Batallion lost 20 officers and 437 men; 4th TA Battalion had by now lost 12 officers and 400 men. *(287,288)*

St Mary's Church, Wargrave (see 1914), re-opened. Except for tower, a new building.

Kendricks Boys' School and Reading School amalgamated. *(126)*

Patrolling in Reading by women police volunteers came to an end because there were too few to do the job properly. Reading Women's Police Patrol Committee organised it. *(115)*

1917. Barkham Road recreation ground, Wokingham, became forage depot for Army.

Some 2,000 Londoners moved to Maidenhead to escape air raids. Some walked all the way, carrying their bedding. *(58)*

Pangbourne College founded by Sir Thomas Lane Devitt and son Philip to educate and train boys for Royal Navy and Merchant Navy. Adjoins Bere Court, where is probably last Chinese wallpaper to come to England. *(299)*

Lady Denman (see 1884) became chairman of National Federation of Women's Institutes (1917-1945). Later founded Denman College at Marcham Park. *(291)*

Elizabeth Frances, 2nd daughter of Sir Henry and Lady Vansittart-Neale of Bisham Abbey, married Major Leo Berkley Paget. *(78)*

Lord Hirst, founder of General Electric Company, bought Foxhill, Reading.

1918. Royal Berkshire Regiment's casualties (August 1915 to November 1918): 3,600. *(287,288)*

Windsor constituency embracing Maidenhead and rural areas began. *(189)*

War Memorial clock erected at Leckhampstead had hands of bayonets, minutes of machinegun ammunition, numerals of rifle ammunition, surrounds of shell cases and chains from battleship. *(291)*

Disabled ex-servicemen bought land at 10s per foot super at California, Wokingham, to start smallholdings scheme. It failed. Most of the land at the turn of the century was owned by the Walters family, including Nine Mile Ride. California was an old hunting lodge on the Ride. District is reputed to have an adder population. *(291)*

William Skindle, founder of Skindles Hotel, died at Worthing aged 101. *(231)*

Reading Police Force given first motor ambulance (see 1889). *(115)*

H.R. Cooper's marble and stone works of Milton (family tradition of stone carving for 200 years) supplied 100 headstones for war cemeteries in France and Belgium, including original headstone for two graves of war casualties buried in St Blaize (patron saint of wool) churchyard, Milton. *(291)*

Government established motor repair depot at Slough. Became known as Slough Dump, because the government's Vehicle Reserve Depot was there. Sold to Slough Trading Company Ltd (1920), became Slough Estates Ltd (1926). About 8,000 employed there. It pioneered similar trading estates in Australia and Canada. Company run by Mr (later Sir Noel) Mobbs. Mr Charles Fairall of Maidenhead developed company's overseas interests. *(428)*

1919. Chief Constable recommended Ford cars (£275 each) for superintendents at Maidenhead, Reading, Wantage, Windsor, Wokingham. The point was made that 'petrol is going down in price but forage for horses at stationary high price'. *(290)*

Lady Astor of Cliveden, Taplow, elected first woman MP (for Plymouth). *(290)*

Windsor's first council houses built in Clewer Avenue. *(189)*

Largest palaeolithic hand axe in UK and probably Europe discovered at Furze Platt, Maidenhead (see 200,000 BC); now in British Museum, replica in Reading Museum. Find led to discovery of Stone Age axe factory nearby, where 589 flint hand axes and tools were subsequently found. European interest in site. *(2,58)*

Motor buses began in Reading. Thames Valley Traction Company began regular services early 1920s. *(114,132,294)*

Canon Drummond, at a meeting of Maidenhead Preventative and Rescue Association, delivered an address decrying the arrival of jazz as an evil that was undermining the strength of the nation. He was widely reported nationally.

Wooden buildings of original Canadian Red Cross Hospital at Cliveden, Taplow sold (see 1914). The chapel fetched £75.

Lady Nancy Astor fined £2 for parking in Maidenhead. *Maidenhead Advertiser* reported: 'The High Street is continually blocked by cars endangering the safety of horses, vehicles and pedestrians'.

1920. Ronald and Arthur Hacker made radio sets in a room in Ray Lea Close, Maidenhead. Their firm eventually became Dynatron Radio Ltd. Broadcasting began in Britain this year. Hackers' sets became the Rolls Royces of radio.

Towing of barges by horses on the Thames ended at about this time. Horses were stabled en route, in riverside shelters called 'hovels'.

Research Institute in Dairying (see 1912) at Reading University became National Institute for Research in Dairying. Institute bought Shinfield Manor (Selengefell: see manors, 1086). National Cattle Breeding Centre established nearby. (Shinfield Grange became University's horticultural centre.) *(114,126)*

1920. Holybrook House, Castle Street, Reading,became training HQ for WEA tutors from all over UK (see 1904). *(124)*

1920. Little girl called Winnie Shotter played the title role at Maidenhead Town Hall in *Little Lord Fauntleroy*. She became Winifred Shotter of the Aldwich farces.

1920c. Wallingford and District Electricity Company began generating current by water wheel from Crowmarsh Mill. When flooding put this out of action, a World War I tank engine was used. *(162)*

Slough Depot (see 1918) sold by Surplus Government Property Disposal Board, including 15,000 motor vehicles. *(428)*

1921. First book produced by Golden Cockerel Press, Waltham St Lawrence, which specialised in fine editions. It was *Adam and Eve and Pinch Me* by A.E. Coppard and was a limited edition of 500 copies. Robert Gibbons, author of *Sweet Thames Run Softly*, was associated with the press and illustrated a number of its books. *(58,276)*

Lord Reading appointed Viceroy of India. Liberal, son of Jewish merchant. Entered Parliament (1904), Attorney General (1910) Lord Chief Justice (1913).

1922. 22 APR. World bell-ringing record set up at Appleton: 21,363 changes (Stedman Caters) in 12 hours 25 minutes. Appleton a centre of campanology (see 1300). *(43)*

1923. Captain Henderson, Reading's Chief Constable, retired. He recommended that the police should be given a motor car to make them more mobile. They received an Austin 12 saloon the following year, which was used principally to carry the new Chief Constable,Thomas Burrows, to ceremonial functions. *(115)*

First MG car built. It had Morris Oxford chassis and Hotchkiss engine. Did 80 mph, won gold medal in Land's End run (1925) driven by Cecil Kimber. Company associated with Abingdon, where (1929) moved to new works and produced first 6-cylinder model. 'MG' are the initials of the Morris Garages. Their racing history began 1930. *(356)*

Steam rollers and lorries massed on Reading Bridge to test maximum weight strain. *(114)*

First application to Ministry for a Maidenhead by-pass. *(492)*

1924. Maidenhead Rowing Club won Thames Cup at Henley Royal Regatta. *(58)*

Earl and Countess of Iveagh opened new premises of National Institute in Dairying at Shinfield (see 1920). *(114)*

Saxon cemetery found at Wallingford. *(162)*

1925. King George V paid private visit to National Institute in Dairying. Childrey had woman blacksmith, who took over from her husband. *(43)*

Plaza Theatre built, Newbury. *(91)*

1926. Caversham Bridge rebuilt. *(126)*

Newbury District Water Company (see 1876) taken over by Corporation, which also took over Newbury Pure Ice and Cold Storage Company Ltd. *(90)*

Australian cricketers opened England tour with a two-day match against minor counties at H.M. Martineau's ground at Holyport.

Reading University got its charter.

Roman Catholic Church in Liebenrood Road, Reading, dedicated to the memory of Hugh Faringdon, last Abbot of Reading, John Rugg, one of his monks, and John Eynon, vicar of St Giles, the Abbot's chief counsellor. *(126)*

Wooden bridge with tollgates replaced at Streatley. *(291)*

1927. Navigation arch of Abingdon Bridge widened. *(293)*

1928. Herbert Henry Asquith buried at Sutton Courtenay. Lived there during premiership (1908-16) and in his retirement. He built The Wharf. *(43,291)*

William Spencer of Cookham died; father of Sir Stanley (artist), Willie (concert pianist), Harold (organist to H.M. Chapel Royal) and Horace ('the variety world's most brilliant failure, playing cards his only possession'). William was musician, poet and naturalist. *(70-73)*

1929. Reading Guild of Artists established. *(114)*

Maidenhead aerodrome licensed at Windsor Road.

28 JUNE. Jealott's Hill Research Station opened. 700 guests present including Belgian Ambassador, Egyptian Prime Minister and leading agriculturalists from all parts of the world. It was to become a repository of all available knowledge of the use of fertilisers in agriculture. Jealott's Hill originally (in Henry IV's time) owned by Roger, alias Jolyf; later Joyliff's Hill and Jealous Hill. Station to make massive contribution to agricultural science. *(359)*

1930. Aldermaston Village Fire Brigade disbanded. The fire alarm bell was in the tower on the inn; the Hind's Head. *(501)*

Marquis of Reading (1860-1935), former Viceroy of India, attended round table conference on future of India at Viceregal Lodge, Delhi. Stella Charnaud (born 1894 Constantinople where her father was with British Foreign Service) attended as his secretary. They married (1931) one year after 1st Lady Reading died (see 1938). *(512)*

RAF Abingdon established.

Sir Denis Burney, designer of the 101 airship (destroyed by fire this year), brought his Streamline Cars Ltd to Cordwallis Estate, Maidenhead (see 1910). There he built the sensational Burney, its' aerodynamic design far in advance of its day, for £1,500. Captain D.M.K. Marandaz followed him with a man called Seelhaft. They made the Marseel, which won more than 250 trials. Its rally drivers included Mr and Mrs A.E. Moss, parents of Stirling Moss. The family lived at Long White Cloud, Bray. *(58,318)*

Restoration of St George's Chapel, Windsor, completed. *(188,189, 191,201)*

Cliveden Set, so-called, began meeting at Cliveden, home of the Astors. *(58)*

Government withdrew consent for the building of the Maidenhead by-pass, under National Economy Act (see 1935). *(492)*

22 DEC. Appleton ringers did it again (see 1922): pulled off second world bell-ringing record. They rang 16,271 changes (Grandsire Caters) in 9 hours 20 mins. *(43)*

First Berkshire Police mobile patrol used 3-wheeled Morgan. Later issued with 900cc motor cycle combinations. Thus the mobile department began. *(290)*

1931. First National Government formed. Lord Reading (Liberal) Foreign Secretary.

1932. Sir Eric Savill created Savill Gardens, Windsor Great Park, one of the finest woodland gardens in UK. They were conceived co-operatively by the King and Queen and Sir Eric and supported by the interest of friends of the royal family who shared their interest in gardening, including the distinguished amateur horticulturalists J.B. Stevenson, Lionel de Rothschild, Sir John Stirling-Maxwell, the Earl of Stair, F.R.S. Balfour, Sir John Ramsden, George Johnstone and Lord Aberconway, for many years president of the Royal Horticultural Society. The gardens were planned on a scale now virtually impossible because of restricting costs. *(199,200)*

1933. John Counsell leased Windsor Theatre (see 1793), which had been turned into a cinema, from Windsor Playhouse Ltd, to start a repertory company. It opened with world premiere of *Clive of India* by William Lipscombe and R.J. Minney. Company began with less than £1,000 capital and Bernard Miles as scenic artist. There was a disappointing response from the public. *(374)*.

1934. Duke and Duchess of York attended Theatre Royal,Windsor,only a few days before it was forced to close. John Counsell got a part in *All Home Comforts* at Fulham Theatre, made a frantic search for backers to re-open the theatre and put all his salary on Windsor Lad. It won, but not enough to re-start the enterprise. *(374)*

Early Saxon cemetery discovered in Saxton Road, Abingdon. *(38)*

Maidenhead Football Club (founded 1869) reached semi-final of the F.A. Amateur Cup.

Ministry of Transport conference on Maidenhead by-pass. Road now described as 'urgent national need'. *(492)*

28 AUG. First issue of *Reading Evening Gazette*.

Edward Terrell OBE QC appointed Recorder of Newbury. He was inventor of plastic armour fitted to ships in World War II. Also invented rocket bomb for attacking U-boat shelters. Among his many publications is *Admiralty Brief – an Autobiography of the War Years. (90)*

1935. Lord Reading, 1st Marquis, died. His widow continued his work for Anglo-American co-operation. He had been Ambassador to Washington.

1936. Maidenhead by-pass route confirmed (see 1935). *(492)*

Maidenhead's car industry closed down. More than 1,000 cars were made on the Cordwallis Estate. *(318)*

Faringdon look-out towers built. Last of the follies.' *(293)*

Trolleybuses replaced motor buses in Reading. *(132)*

Edward VIII's abdication speech delivered from Fort Belvedere, Sunningdale, which he had used as his country home when Prince of Wales. It was here that the abdication order was signed. *(189)*

1937. Slough Community Centre opened on Trading Estate, initiated by Mr Noel Mobbs. First of its kind in the world. Membership grew to 5,000. *(428)*

Parliamentary Bill for new Thames Bridge to carry Maidenhead by-pass (see 1936). *(492)*

Furze Platt Halt, Maidenhead, opened. Used by between 5,000 and 10,000 passengers daily.

1938. Stella, Lady Reading, founded Women's Voluntary Service (WVS). Previously at heart of Personal Service League formed during depression in 1930s to help unemployed and their families with clothes &c. She wrote memorandum on which WVS was based, from which sprung Meals on Wheels service for elderly, home helps scheme and other services later to be part of Welfare State. WVS became Britain's most remarkable public service. Became Women's Royal Voluntary Service (1966). Regional HQ set up at Reading. Helped local authorities prepare Air Raid Precautions (ARP) schemes. First aid and gas defence classes held at Lady Reading's home. This was the time of Munich and of impending disaster. *(65)*

Home Park, Windsor, handed over to Borough Council 'for the benefits of the inhabitants of Windsor and district'. The idea was Queen Victoria's. *(189)*

Theatre Royal, Windsor, re-opened by John Counsell and Mary Kerridge, whom he had married. First production: *Dear Brutus.* King George VI told a dinner guest at the Castle: 'I know the chap who is running it. He used to be at my camp'. Six weeks later the King and Queen (formerly Duke and Duchess of York) attended, to see *The Rose Without a Thorn. (274)*

Horace Smith of Holyport began giving riding lessons to Princess

Elizabeth and Princess Margaret. The princesses were learning to ride side-saddle. *(83)*

Thames Valley Eggs Ltd distributed 866 million eggs. Grew from local domestic industry. It had long been a cottage industry. *(291,310)*

1939. County began war preparations. Gasmasks and air raid shelters appeared and everyone with a piece of land began to dig: either slit trenches or for food production. Sticky tape went on windows to stop glass splintering from bomb blast, women made blackout curtains. Cardboard coffins for gas victims stored in chalk caves at Emmer Green, along with archives from Reading. *(291)*

Wantage took up its tram lines. Elsewhere, railings and metal of all kinds fed into munitions manufacture.

Reading Evening Gazette ceased publication.

Construction of Maidenhead by-pass optimistically began. Cost: £80,000 a mile. Bulldozers a new construction tool used for first time in East Berks. *(492)*

Women's Voluntary Service begin billeting of evacuees from London and help with food control and rationing; set up mobile food and welfare food services in villages, distributed clothes, pioneered Meals on Wheels service for elderly. 6,000 children, mothers and expectant mothers in first wave of evacuees from London to Maidenhead. Two residential schools and their staffs followed. *(65)*

Queen Wilhelmina of Holland and Dutch bodyguard evacuated from Holland to Stubbings House, Maidenhead. King Haakon of Norway evacuated to Folijohn Park, Fifield. Princess Juliana also stayed at Maidenhead. King Peter of Yugoslavia, the Grand Duchess of Luxembourg and King Zog of Albania moved to Ascot. *(58,290)*

Little ships from the Thames sailed away to Dunkirk to bring back part of the British Expeditionary Force, among them Geoffrey Messum of Bray and other local boat owners. He brought home 22 Frenchmen and one Englishman. *(58)*

1940. Air Transport Auxiliary (ATA) set up at White Waltham and began ferrying planes to operational bases. De Havillands constructed the aerodrome before ATA's arrival, as an elementary training school. Land is part of Shottesbrooke Estate, which has come down intact from Saxon times and is home of John Smith, last High Steward of Maidenhead. ATA was born from an idea by Gerard d'Erlanger. Among the civilian ferry pilots from all over the world were young girls in their 20s, who ferried unarmed four-engine bombers. Many pilots lost their lives. Later, the Duke of Edinburgh was to learn to fly here. *(69)*

Camp for German prisoners-of-war set up at Kimbers, Maidenhead. Showboat, Oldfield Road, former club, became services club for airmen and ATA personnel. *(58)*

Home Guard (began as Local Defence Volunteers) on anti-parachute duty throughout the county and ran river patrols on the Thames.

British Restaurants (so-called) were opened for cheap meals and staffed by WVS.

1940. Bomber Command airfield opened at Chilton. *(291)*

Reformed Synagogue set up at No 9 Boyn Hill, Maidenhead, through Hugo Schwab for Jewish community, many of whom were evacuees from London bombing. *(58)*

Greenham airfield built for US Air Force gliders. *(90)*

German prisoner-of-war camp established at Stanbury, Spencers Wood. *(291)*

1941. Bisham Abbey used as convalescent home for VAD Nurses and Red Cross. It also housed evacuees, and troops of the special defence battalion for London were stationed there. *(78)*

National Fire Service Formed, out of which came Berkshire and Reading Fire authority (1948). This signalled the end of the county's volunteer brigades.

United States Air Force took over Greenham Common and established bomber base there: the B47 Bomber Wing. *(90)*

1942. Deer removed from Windsor Great Park. There were 1,000 there in 1649. The herd had descended from German stock imported by Charles II and they were the biggest red deer in any English park. But blackout conditions of World War II and the fact that the park was used for food production made the deer a hazard. Englefield Park still has a herd of 100-150. *(189)*

Lord Astor made over Cliveden, with certain of its contents and works of art, the gardens, grounds and Cliveden Reach of the Thames, to the National Trust, with an endowment. *(63)*

1943. 10 FEB. Reading's only air raid in World War II. One stick of bombs fell on Wellsteeds Store, The People's Pantry and the Post Office. The town was used to try out Snock (a kind of fish), wooden-soled shoes, cormorants' eggs and Chinese dehydrated eggs. *(114)*

Station Road, Newbury, bombed. Council schools, St John's Church and 10 almshouses destroyed; 294 homes damaged; 15 people killed. Eight bombs were dropped. *(90)*

BBC monitoring station set up at Caversham Park.

1944. Maidenhead WVS ran welcome Club for American troops. *(65)*

King and Queen visited Maidenhead Thicket to inspect the ploughed-up acres which were part of the Ministry of Agriculture's Grow More Food Campaign.

1945. At Cliveden (see 1914) the Canadian War Memorial Hospital replaced Lord Astor's World War I Hospital. Built by Canadian Government at cost of £5m, it was handed to National Trust (1946) as War Memorial. During 1939-45 war, 25,068 men were tended there. During the war 1,650 bombs fell in the Maidenhead area. Of these, 1,500 were incendiaries. One flying bomb (Doodle bug) fell in Cookham Road garden. Sixty-two people were slightly injured. One man had his leg broken when an unfused bomb came through his roof at Furze Platt. *(58)*

Treasures from London Museums stored in underground chambers at Knowl Hill. (Later designated as administrative centre in event of nuclear attack and scene of demonstration by Nuclear Disarmament Movement.)

During the war, Aldermaston Court was training centre for women's services. Princess Elizabeth learned to drive there. *(501)*

Lord Desborough of Taplow Court died aged 89. *(58)*

British Telecommunications Research Ltd moved to Taplow Court. Its research and development laboratories sponsored by British Insular Callender's Cables Ltd and Automatic Telephone and Electric Co Ltd.

1946. Harwell became Atomic Energy Centre. Its staff was housed in Abingdon, Wantage, Wallingford and Didcot. They occupied some 1,400 houses, and being research scientists and engineers, they brought high academic standards to the area: there were streets where so many doctorates lived, that plain misters were in the minority. This high concentration brought great social changes, which challenged local authorities to provide many new schools and other services. Sir John Cockroft first scientist in charge. *(293,376,377)*

Atomic Energy Research Establishment opened at Chilton and brought piped water to the village, which previously had only a village pump. Chilton's downland nurseries famous for orchids and specialised in Lady Slipper. Steeplechasing training establishment on the Chilton Mile. *(291)*

Berkshire's borough police forces and the Berkshire County Constabulary consolidated into one Berkshire Force. *(290)*

Reading Blue Coat School moved to Holme Park, Sonning. A pupil, Seth Wisdom, patented method of fitting false teeth without extracting old stumps. Set up Reading Atmospheric Tooth Company, which became Globe Artificial Teeth Institute. *(114)*

1947. Princess Elizabeth received Freedom of the Borough of Windsor. She said at ceremony: 'this town, whose name my family bears, is very dear to me. Indeed, I regard it as home in a way no other place can be'. *(189)*

New Faculty of Letters begun at Whiteknights, Reading. Whiteknights was bought from the Goldsmid family with government grant help. It covers 300 acres (see 1849). *(114)*

Nat. Inst. for Dairying took over Hall Farm, Arborfield (see 1924). Major flood disaster in Thames Valley towns, following heavy snowfall and quick thaw. Biggest flood since 1894. More than 100 families evacuated from Maidenhead. Beds set up in Town Hall. Army called in to help. WVS ran food deliveries to stranded families. Thames Valley became a disaster area. Commonwealth countries sent aid to victims; funds established to replace lost furniture etc. Lord Mayor of London visited Maidenhead to inspect damage. RAF helped dry out homes with special machines. Led to conference of Thames mayors on flood prevention and to Thames 'by-pass' flood relief channel at Maidenhead, where flooding was fairly frequent. No attempt had been made to tackle the problem since Mayor Norkett's dam disaster in 1914.

Vandervell Products began building Maidenhead factory. Here, bearings for cars all over the world are made and the famous racing car, the Vanwall, was developed by Tony Vandervell.

Easthampstead Park, former seat of Marquess of Downshire, seriously damaged by fire. Had been bought by Berks County Council and became teachers' training centre. *(290)*

At Greenham Common, Inspector F.E. Francis fired on by gunman at point-blank range after he had made an arrest, but refused to release him. Gunman escaped in police car. Arrested after 70/80 mph chase to Chiswick. *(290)*

Sunninghill Park, a wartime RAF base and the intended home of Princess Elizabeth and Lieutenant Philip Mountbatten, destroyed by fire. Fourteen brigades failed to save it. Subsequently demolished. *(290)*

Police Sergeant Speller solved robbery at Calcot through foot-print by crepe-soled shoe which was photographed by Sergeant Ingram. Believed to be first case of its kind. Facts published in *Police Journal* October-November 1949. *(290)*

Slough Industrial Health Service set up. *(428)*

Miss Phyllis Vansittart-Neale loaned Bisham Abbey to Central Council for Physical Recreation as memorial to her two nephews, Berkeley and Guy Paget, who were killed in World War II. Became Britain's first national sports centre. *(87)*

Skindles Hotel, Maidenhead, severely damaged by fire.

1948. Mrs Freeman Lee (88) murdered in her home in Ray Park Avenue, Maidenhead. Became known as the Maidenhead Trunk Murder. George Russell was hanged for the crime. *(290)*

1948. Bert Bushnell of Maidenhead and Richard Burnett of Sonning won gold medal in Olympic Double Sculls. *(58)*

Letcombe Bassett, the watercress village, foiled an attempt to rehouse the villagers at Letcombe Regis. It had been called a rural slum. *(43)*

First working boat on Kennet and Avon Canal for more than 20 years returned to Newbury from Avonmouth in eight days, with 10 tons of grain. It encouraged John Gould of Newbury to buy a pair of working boats, 'Colin' and 'Iris'. There was little traffic , but enthusiasts were looking for a revival. *(279)*

Denman College opened as adult education centre by Nat.Fed. W I, which bought Marcham Park. Institutes raised £60,000 in 3 years towards purchase price.Carnegie U K Trust gave grant. *(291)*

Bracknell designated a new town, with an area of 1,870 acres. Fierce opposition from farming interests, on ground that good agricultural land would be lost. *(504)*

Beginning of the Development Age. Berkshire's Development Plan was one of first in country to be approved by the Ministry. Rebuilding, especially in East Berks, concentrated on clearing slums and removing the waiting list for council houses, but there was still a shortage of materials; building was licensed. Overcrowding by wartime evacuees, many of whom stayed, was at the heart of the housing problem, plus the fact that no house had been built for six years. *(142,499)*

1950. John Wolfenden (later Sir John) appointed Vice-Chancellor of Reading University, formerly head of Shrewsbury and Uppingham. Chaired national committee on homosexuality and prostitution. *(114)*
Reading Christian Council Arts Festival. It was the first time that all Reading's churches had combined as one body for a common end. *(126)*
Atomic Weapons Research Establishment opened at Aldermaston. Short announcement by Ministry of Supply. All roads crossing the Establishment's area permanently closed for security reasons. *(Mercury 3.6.50)*

1951. Early Saxon finds at Kingsbury, Old Windsor. Full scale dig over 20 acres by Dr Brian Hope-Taylor established site of Saxon Palace. Present house, The White Hermitage, believed to occupy site of important central building. Site occupied for five or six centuries before Roman occupation. Finds included fragments of glass, iron keys, two coins (Henry I) and large sophisticated water mill, the only Saxon watermill of its type ever found. A canal, nearly three-quarters of a mile long had been dug to provide the water power. *(507)*
Princess Elizabeth opened restored Windsor guildhall. *(189)*

AUG. First buildings completed and first homes occupied in Bracknell New Town. *(502,504)*
Kennet & Avon Canal Association formed, dedicated to completing restoration of the canal connecting London with Bristol. The occasional traffic of 1948 had stopped, locks were padlocked because of deterioration in the canal. John Gould (see 1948), whose contract to carry loads of turf spit from Hampton-on-Thames had ended, issued a writ against the British Transport Commission to enforce its statutory obligation to keep the canal open. Both he and John Knill (who was carrying salt from Cerebos Ltd, Cheshire, into Newbury) were caught en route by the closure. Court awarded John Gould £5,000 damages. Long struggle to open canal began. *(278-280)*

1952. Coleshill House destroyed by fire. It was the first house in the classic manner to dispense with pilasters and columns. Stables and dovecot survived. *(291,299)*
Sulhampstead House became the headquarters of the new Berkshire Constabulary. *(291)*
Maidenhead's collection of town plate begun. *(66)*
Berkshire Police began using radio. *(290)*
Abingdon Unicorn Theatre performed in delightful Tudor building which was once the home of the owner of Abbey Mills (see 1400). *(38)*
Desborough estates dissolved. They covered 12,000 acres of Maidenhead (see 1945). *(58)*

28 APR. Berkshire Development Plan drawn up by County Planning Department was one of first such plans to receive government approval. For first time, every acre in county zoned for future use. Protection of rural areas from development, such as Vale of White Horse, security for farming etc. This was the beginning of planning permission.

1954. US Air Force base at Greenham Common, war-time bomber station from this year accommodated the 3909 Combat Support Group (Strategic Air Command). The station was rebuilt to take this NATO Air Force.

1955. National Institute for Research in Dairying built on site of Arborfield Hall. Manor dates from Norman times. First Lord was Bulwe of Edburgfield.

1956. The Great Barn, Great Coxwell, Faringdon (see 1204), bequeathed to National Trust by Mr E.E. Cook. Once the property of the Pleydell-Bouverie family and part of Coleshill Estate (see 1768). *(420)* Abingdon Town Hall re-opened by the Queen after restoration. Ministry of Works began scheme in 1952. *(38,42)*

1957. Cookham Lock rebuilt. *(495)*

1958. Letcombe Laboratory established to study agricultural aspects of environmental contamination with radio-active substances. Some re-orientation (1963) to research plant nutrition and relationships between root systems and the soil.

George Appleton, formerly of Holmanleaze, Maidenhead, former pupil of East Street elementary school and Maidenhead Grammar School (now Desborough), Archbishop of Perth, Western Australia, appointed second Anglican Bishop in Jerusalem.

1959. Clifton Hampden Bridge held largest colony of house martins in British Isles: more than 400 nests. Mentioned in Robert Gibbons *Till I end My Song*. Colony built up over several years: 1939 – 128 nests; 1954–450. Bridge scheduled by Nature Conservancy as site of scientific interest. (It was designed by Sir George Gilbert Scott 1864 and built from local bricks.) *(43)*

Wallingford Great Western Railway branch line closed.

New television cartoon character 'Torchy' appeared, the product of AP Films Ltd of Islet Park, Maidenhead. Their science-fiction puppet films, notably 'Fireball XL5', 'Captain Scarlet' etc., achieved world-wide acclaim. Gerry Anderson, Arthur Provis, Reg Hill, Sylvia Thamm and John Read began firm.

Contracts for Maidenhead by-pass approved. Construction began in May. The ghost road cleared in 1939, when work stopped, was partially overgrown. Road now part of the M4 (South Wales Motorway). The bridge piles for the Thames crossing were put up before original contract ended. Engineers now began to redesign the longest all-welded steel span in the country, to contain 700 tons of steel and 1,000 cubic yards of concrete. Its overall length 348ft with a clear span of 270ft across the water and width 100ft. Each span was fabricated by Horseley Bridge & Thomas Piggott Ltd of Tipton, Staffs, at their factory. Design was by Freeman Fox & Partners. Sections were site-welded. The welders undertook similar test operations and only after rigid tests and x-ray examinations of their work were two squads of three men approved for the job. The M4 began on the drawing board in the 1930s as the South Wales Orbital Road. *(492)*

World's first helicopter airliner built at Maidenhead by Fairey Aviation, which took over the old ATA premises at White Waltham (see 1940). Nearby was established West London Aero Club. Its instructor, Flight Captain Miss Joan Hughes, had ferried bombers for ATA as a young girl. *(58)*

1960. Satellite Tracking and Data Acquisition Station established at Winkfield on a site used by the Radio Research Station, Slough. Similar stations are distributed round the world and linked by teleprinter, voice and data circuits to NASA's Goddard Space Flight Centre, USA. The functions of the network of stations, for which Winkfield is equipped are to track and collect by radio scientific information from unmanned satellites, and to issue commands to satellites carrying scientific payloads (see 1973). *(427)*

Baron Iliffe of Yattendon of Basildon Park, benefactor of Coventry Cathedral, vice-chairman of Birmingham Post and Mail Ltd, chairman of *Coventry Evening Telegraph* and *Cambridge News*, succeeded to the barony.

1961. Meteorological Office moved from Dunstable to Bracknell where they write the scripts for BBC sound and television weather programmes and provide the broadcasters who make the weather forecasts.

Maidenhead by-pass opened in June (see 1959). *(492)*

Civic Trust Facelift project for Windsor. The Queen, Prince Philip and 500 mayors celebrated completion of the scheme.

Residents of Northcourt, once part of Abingdon Abbey, and students of the Atomic Energy Research Establishment converted old tithe barn (1720) into church called Christ Church. Pulpit made from stones of old abbey watermill. Consecrated by Bishop of Oxford 25 November. *(291)*

Ceiling of St Mary's Church, Maidenhead, began to fall on congregation. It had been declared to be one of the largest unsupported roof spans. Services transferred and fund opened to build new church. *(58)*

Service of exorcism at Purley Hall, said to be haunted by ghost of Warren Hastings and Grey Lady. *(291)*

1962. Duke of Kent began flying instruction at White Waltham.

25 JUNE. Maidenhead's new town hall opened by the Queen. Built in grounds of former Manor of Ive. Old town hall (1777) demolished and tower block erected on site. New building designed by local architect Guy North. Central Area Redevelopment scheme, including pedestrianised High Street, plans by Lord Esher, approved about this time. *(66)*

The Louis Baylis (*Maidenhead Advertiser*) Charitable Trust formed, which in effect gave the *Maidenhead Advertiser* (see 1869) to the town of Maidenhead.

Stanley Spencer Gallery opened at Cookham. Sir Stanley (1891-1959) spent virtually whole life at Cookham, rated among greatest living artists of his day. Knighted 1959. Greatest work the murals at the Oratory of All Souls, Burghclere (1933). *(70-74)*

1963. Designated area of Bracknell New Town extended by 1,400 acres to accommodate an estimated population of 60,000. *(504)*

Central Council for Physical Recreation bought Bisham Abbey from Mrs Elizabeth Paget (see 1947) to perpetuate its use for the youth of England. The remaining furniture and pictures were bought from her cousin and successor, Miss M.E. Dickinson of Bisham Grange (1965). *(78)*

Passenger receipts at Maidenhead Station, according to the Beeching Report, exceeded £25,000 pa.

1964. Maidenhead awarded European flag by assembly of Council of Europe, in recognition of services for the ideal of European Unity. *(58,66)*

Berlin Steglitz named a street Maidenhead Allee.

1965. Maidenhead goods station closed. Coal yards established there moved to Taplow station. Later, Ford Motor Company took over the yard as railhead.

Council for British Archaeology included Abingdon in its list of 51 towns 'so splendid and so precious that ultimate responsibility for them should be a national concern'. *(37,45)*

Landmark Trust, a sort of min-National Trust, formed by John and Christian Smith of Shottesbrooke Park, Maidenhead.

1966. Windsor and Eton Relief Road and new river bridge, Elizabeth Bridge, completed. *(189)*

Kennet and Avon Canal Trust (which K & A Association became in 1962) rebuilt bridge at Bridge Street, Reading. Trust also rebuilt Sulhamstead Lock with help of prisoners from Oxford. Canal now open 8½ miles from Reading. At Newbury, 11 miles open to navigation. *(278,279)*

Abingdon Council opened new 500-seat Abbey Hall.

Colleges of Further Education began courses for craft apprentices, under Industrial Training Act. Extensive rebuilding and re-equipping at colleges over past few years. Cost met by industry. New Act worked through Training Boards. Cost per student: £300 pa. *(294)*

Bracknell's new fire station completed. Cost: £300,000.

Meetings all over county as change to comprehensive education for 70,000 children in 300 schools began. 'Hands off grammar schools' now rarely heard. Education Director, T.D.W. Whitfield, said majority of parents were neutral.

Berkshire (population 447,950) now fastest growing county in England. Population increase estimated at 15,000 a year. Businesses and industries prosperous. Unemployment virtually unknown: in East Berks there were seven vacant jobs to every unemployed person. One of the catchment areas for population flow from Northern England and out of Greater London. School places required annually equal to about five comprehensive schools. Housing waiting lists all over county lengthening. Proximity of London Airport and speedy M4 motoring brought pressure on East Berks housing. Clamour for development and planning control of rural areas put county in front line of the Battle of the Development Age. Other pressures came from anticipated European trade with Common Market and expectation that connecting road from North with proposed Channel Tunnel would pass through East Berks, thus making it, with M4, the cross-roads of Southern England. *(294)*

1967. Reading Guild of the Arts formed by Rotary Club. *(114,126)* Gilbert Beale of Basildon died. He created riverside park and Child-Beale Trust (now associated with Wildlife Trust). *(291)* Production methods of *Newbury Weekly News* filmed for exhibition in newly-developed African countries. The *Newbury Weekly News* previously subject of film by war-time Crown Film Unit. *(90)*

1968. Thames Valley Police Authority formed: Berks, Bucks and Oxon County forces and Reading and Oxford City forces merged. Headquarters Kidlington, Oxford.
Abingdon Market Place ceased to be used for town fairs. In Middle Ages, St Mary's Fair in connection with the abbey's patronal festival was one of the most important in England (see 1348). *(38)*

1969. Maidenhead High Steward's Barge moored at Maidenhead Bridge. Formerly belonged to Jesus College. Bought by John Smith, high steward, beautifully restored; art work by John Pockett of Cookham, folk art expert. *(58)*
Alexander Chapel built at Cranbourne in memory of Field Marshall Earl Alexander of Tunis, whose home was nearby. *(291)*
Braywick House became world headquarters of Pandair Freight Limited. Said to be haunted by White Lady (see 1773). *(64)*
Windsor's Ward Royal, a fortress-like complex of flats and maisonettes, won diploma for design from Ministry of Housing and Local Government, but not from the locals, among whom it created considerable controversy, some believing it to be a new prison. *(189)*

1970. Windsor Bridge declared unsafe and closed to traffic. *(189)*
Kingston Bagpuize celebrated its millenium with historical pageant presented by the Women's Institute. First recorded charter 907. Name derives from the Norman family of Bachepuise; many different spellings. *(291,319)*
Commemorative Post Office stamp marking centenary of Astronomical Society carried picture of Francis Baily, son of former mayor of Newbury, William Herschel of Slough, who discovered planet Uranus, and his son John Herschel, who was said to have been educated at Newbury. *(90)*
New buildings at Denman College (see 1948) opened by Queen Elizabeth the Queen Mother. They included craft rooms. There are more than 4,000 students a year and more than 200 courses.

1971. 22 DEC. M4 through Berkshire opened. Until now Reading had through vehicle flow of 25,000 daily. *(294)*
Mr Richard Seymour, chairman of Berkshire County Council, handed to Mr W.A. Hedges a single rose. It was, as requested by Mr Hedges, a

token rent for a car park and picnic site at Wittenham Clumps. Hedges family also gave public access to 100 acres. Clumps have Iron Age Hill Fort.

Billy Smart's circus ended summer touring, to concentrate on Windsor Safari Park. Winter quarters at St George's stables, Cranbourne, where is life-sized statue of Billy Smart by Edwin Russell in forecourt. *(291)*

King's Cup Air Race took off from White Waltham Aerodrome.

Memorial window unveiled at Church of St James the Greater, Eastbury, dedicated to poet Edward Thomas (1878-1917). Contributions came from 700 people worldwide. The window was engraved by Lawrence Whistler. Thomas wrote books and poems on the English countryside. He was killed in action at Assas in World War I. His wife Helen (1877-1967) published biographical volumes. *(291)*

Park Place, Remenham, became a boarding school for handicapped boys in the area of the Hillingdon education authority. *(291)*

1972. State visit to Windsor by Queen Juliana of the Netherlands. *(189)*

English Rugby team also Olympic hockey, canoeing and weight-lifting teams, trained at the National Recreation Centre, Bisham Abbey, which is under the umbrella of the National Sports Council. *(78)*

Local Government Act of this year wiped out rural district and urban district councils and set up a two-tier system of local government organised into new areas, called districts. All Berkshire councils went into the melting pot. They were poured into a mould which produced six district councils as second-tier authorities, with the county council as the top tier. At the same time, county boundaries were revised nationally so that the new districts would have high populations. Berkshire lost its historic Vale of the White Horse to Oxfordshire and with it the 'White Horse' symbol.

1973. First elections for the new local authorities held. They then worked in double harness with the old authorities for a year.

Radio and Space Research Station, Slough, renamed Appleton Laboratory. it became the Radio Research Station of the Department of Scientific and Industrial Research. It became a separate establishment in 1948. It was a natural continuation of the work of Sir William Herschell (see 1786). This year it was amalgamated with the former Astrophysics Research Unit at Culham. it also organised collaboration with the universities, giving advice and support for their research and advising in such matters as frequency allocation and radio interference. It is also exploring the potential of millimetre waves for new communications networks (see 1960). *(427)*

Mr Bernard Theobald at Westbury Farm, Purley, set up a commercial vineyard from German and French stock, following tradition of the Romans' Thames Valley vineyards and those of abbots of Reading. Mr Theobald was the first man in England to grow classic Bordeaux grapes. His red wine, made from the Burgundy Pinot Noire grape, is first commercial wine produced in England since 1914. Main winery and bottling plant in Elizabethan barn. *(505)*

Maidenhead Central Library, designed by Paul Koralek, opened by Prince Richard of Gloucester. Wide publicity in architectural press. Many visitors from overseas: Germany, Scandinavia etc. Exterior design produced local controversy. Mr James Powell librarian. Library largest book selection in Berkshire. *(490)*

1974. 1 APR. Reorganised local government came into operation. The Mayor of the new Royal Borough of Windsor and Maidenhead (Councillor Kit Aston) approached the Palace, and the Queen agreed to make a river journey through the new borough from Hurley to Magna Carta Island, as the river Thames was one factor common to the whole area. The journey was to be an encouragement to the new borough to think of itself as one unit.

18 OCT. The journey was made in pouring rain, but thousands turned out in towns and villages as the flotilla of boats escorting the Queen moved with split-second timing over the whole route. Her Majesty came ashore at towns and villages. There were presentations all along the way and on board the Queen's launch. *(491)*

1974. Windsor Free Pop Festival described by Chief Constable David Holdsworth as 'squalid, dirty and drug-infested'. He reported: 'the first thing to be clear about is that the events which took place in Windsor Great Park in 1972, 1973 and 1974 had very little to do with music – not even pop music; and they were not pop festivals . . . the advertised principal ingredients of the Windsor festivals were social and political protest, drugs and sexual licence'. All were unlawful. *(506)*

Commonwealth War Graves Commission headquarters, built in Marlow Road, Maidenhead, won Royal Institute of British Architects' award for good design. Presented by the Hon David Smith, HM Lieutenant for Berkshire.

Foundation stone laid for £1¾ million sports hall at National Sports Council's centre at Bisham Abbey. Sophisticated indoor facilities for major team and court games (see 1963).

1975. Craft centres established at Ardington in attempt to bring new life into slumbering village. *(339,505)*

Prince of Wales became High Steward of Royal Borough of Windsor and Maidenhead.

Wantage opened new Civic Hall. *(168)*

1976. Councillor Euphemia Underhill, last mayor of the old Borough of Maidenhead, and her husband, Commander Lewis Underhill RN (rtd), guests of honour during American bi-centennial celebrations at Lawrenceville (formerly Maidenhead), New Jersey. This was the first official link between Maidenhead, Berkshire, and Maidenhead, USA.

John Smith of Shottesbrooke Park, Maidenhead, appointed HM Lieutenant for Berkshire. He was High Steward of Maidenhead 1967-1974 and made first Honorary Freeman of the new Royal Borough of Windsor and Maidenhead in 1975.

St Mary's, Wallingford, tower restored at cost of £48,000. (First tower destroyed by lightning 1638 and rebuilt with stone from old Wallingford Castle.) *(161,162)*

Twyford Mill burned down. Originally a silk mill founded by two brothers from Macclesfield (1810), later flour mill and finally a cattle-cake producing plant.

Thames Valley Broadcasting Ltd began local radio in Berkshire at 6 am on 8 March with a broadcast by Paul Hollingdale.

B R high-speed train began its regular runs through Berkshire. *(294)*

1977. Silver Jubilee Year. County's major celebrations centred on Windsor, which coincided with Windsor's 700th civic anniversary (see 1277). Town jammed with people and traffic for Windsor Great Park bonfire, which was started by the Queen and was signal for chain of fire across UK and Commonwealth. Worldwide television hook-up. Probably first time the Queen had ever been late for an engagement.

Councillor Kit Aston, organiser of Royal Borough's Jubilee celebrations, launched Queen's Trees Scheme for replanting part of Thames Valley. Prince Philip planted first tree in Windsor Great Park.

New Maidenhead Fire Station opened. Maidenhead Hospital closed.

Big new Courage Brewery complex under construction at Reading.

Greatest coin find in UK this century at Waltham St Lawrence, by songwriter Bill Parkinson of Essex and wife Jenny. Consisted of 58 gold or Belgic coins; 142 pre-Roman silver coins and 23 Roman silver denarii, some republican, dated from about 250-30 BC and the end of the 2nd century AD. At least 12 of the Celtic coins believed minted at Calleva (Silchester). Only five coins of this kind previously known to exist (see 100 BC). There were 52 gold coins of the British Atrebates tribe minted between about 30 BC and 46 AD; most of silver coins also from Atrebates period. Four gold coins were from Ambiami tribe, imported from the continent, dating from 30 BC. Others included five extremely rare coins from King Apaticum period, minted in Colchester. There is a Roman temple site nearby, where coins and pottery of the late Roman period have been found.

1978. Government ordered investigation into 12 cases of plutonium contamination at Aldermaston Atomic Research plant. Sir Edward Pochin, one of the world's leading authorities on radiology, investigated health and safety standards at the plant. *(Guardian* 18.8.78)

Basildon Park, near Streatley, presented to National Trust by Lord Iliffe. Classical Georgian House and 400 acres of park and woodland. Building work began (1776) for Sir Francis Sykes, who made his fortune with the East India Company and was associated with Clive and Warren Hastings. Architect was John Carr of York. Lord and Lady Iliffe bought Basildon in 1952.

The Queen and Duke of Edinburgh opened Reading's new civic centre and attended performance by Reading's Youth Orchestra at the Hexagon; also visited Thames Valley Broadcasting Station.

8 FEB. The Hon Gordon Palmer, Vice Lieutenant of Berkshire, succeeded Mr John Smith as Her Majesty's Lord Lieutenant of Berks.

104

BIBLIOGRAPHY

Pre-history and early arrivals

1. Guide to Prehistoric England	Nicholas Thomas	
2. Lower Palaeolithic Archaeology in Britain	J. Wymer	
3. Britain's Structure and Scenery	L. Dudley Stamp	1966
4. The Pre-Historic Ridgeway	Patrick Crampton	1962
5. Ice Ages: their nature and effect	Ian Cornwall	
6. The Normans and their myth	R.H.C. Davis	1976
7. The Green Roads of England	R. Hippisley Cox	1914
8. White Horse Hill	L.V. Grinsell	
9. The Icknield Way	Edward Thomas	
10. Oxoniensia XV: Celtic Field Systems on the Berkshire Downs	P.P. Rhodes	
11. Anglo-Saxon Burials in the Middle Thames	Luke Over	
12. Romano-British Settlement in Thames Valley	Luke Over	
13. Romano-British Influence in the Maidenhead Area	Luke Over	
14. An Analysis and List of Berkshire Barrows	L.V. Grinsell	
15. The Romano-British Site on Lowbury Hill	Donald Atkinson	
16. Iron Age Communities	Barry Cunliffe	1974
17. Domesday Book (fascimile)		
18. Victorian County History of Berkshire		
19. The Archaeology of Berkshire	Harold J.E. Peake	1931
20. The Roman Town of Calleva Atrebatum	George C. Boon	1957
21. The History and Antiquities of Silchester (1857)		
22. Place Names in Berkshire	F.M. Stenton	1911
23. Oxford Dictionary of Place Names	Eilert Ekwall	1960
24. English Place Names	Kenneth Cameron	1977
25. Topographical & Statistical Description of Berks	G.A. Cooke	1802
26. Soils of Berkshire	N.H. Pizer	1931
27. The Berkshire Ridgeway	Francis Jones	1949

Local Histories

Cloth Trade

Coaching

Civil War

Waterways

General

Journals

484.   Didcot, Newbury and Southampton Railway (T.B. Sands) Feb
       Mar 1955
485.   Maidenhead Brunel's Bridge Mar Apr 1949

Newspapers
486.   Whiteknights Estate *Reading Mercury 1904*
487.   Reading Standard Souvenir Number (1898-1923)
488.   Reading Mercury Hist. Supplement 1923
489.   Windsor Express 150th Anniversary Supplement 1962
490.   Maidenhead Library - Maidenhead Advertiser Supplement
       1973
491.   Queen's Thames Journey 1974 - Md Advtr Supplement
492.   Maidenhead by-pass - Advertiser Supplement 1961
493.   Windsor Project Souvenir - Windsor Express 1961
494.   Maidenhead Advertiser January 21, 1891
495.   Municipal Journal 15 November 1957
496.   Bradfield College - Illustrated London News 1959
497.   Arms and Armour at Ockwells Manor - Connoisseur Feb 1905
498.   Staff Journal, Mid-Southern Water Co. 1975

499. History of Berkshire County Council: MS	E.R. Davies	
500. Wallingford Pageant broadcast script, 25 November 1951	County Library	
501. Aldermaston Jubilee Brochure	W.A. Cox	1977
502. Bracknell Before the New Town (pamphlet)	Lee Pooley	1976
503. Maidenhead Cottage Hospital Annual Report 1880.		
504. Bracknell (Development Corporation pamphlets)		
505. Out and About (pub. Maidenhead Advertiser)	Ed. David Ranger	1977
506. The New Society (pamphlet)	Thames Valley Police	

Maps

Ordnance Survey
Ancient Britain South Sheet
Britain in Dark Ages
Roman Britain
Stansford's Map of River Thames

Berkshire County Library, Reading
Barkshire described, J. Speed (1611) 15" X 20"
Barke Shire, J. Bill (1626) from the Abridgement of Camden's
Britannia.

A new map of Barkshire, W. Hollar 14½" X 19½" in Antiquities of Barkshire (E. Ashmole) 1719.

A map of Berkshire with its hundreds, R. Blome 7¼" X 12" (in Britannia or a Geographical Description of England by R. Blome 1673).

Berk Shire, R. Morden 13½" X 16" (1695) from Camden's *Britannia*.

Barkshire, H. Moll 7¼" X 9½" (1724) from a set of 50 new and correct maps of the counties of England and Wales.

A new map of the County of Berks 17¼" X 19½" from Smith's new British Atlas 1804. J. Cary

Ditto corrected to 1832 showing parliamentary divisions.

Maps of the County of Berks from actual survey, C & J Greenwood 21" X 25¾", from atlas of the counties of England 1834.

Norden's Map of Windsor Forest. J. Norden 1858

Plan of the River Lodden and intended navigable canal from Basingstoke to River Thames near Monkey Island 1769.

Plan of Thames and intended canal from Reading to Monkey Island 1771.

Map of the navigations by the rivers and canals west of London. Z. Allnutt 1810

Commencement of the roads to Bath and Bristol. R. Laurie and J. Whittle.

Maps of principal towns.

Maps and surveys of farms (1771) in Beckett, Shrivenham, Standwick. Viscount Barrington.

The local collection at Reading Library contains a large quantity of private papers, unpublished MSS, newspaper cuttings and reports, all indexed under subject and author in the library's catalogue. Reading Museum has the Silchester Collection and display and an extensive collection of local pre-historic finds. The County Record Office has large collection of family documents, charters, maps and records. It is also the repository of official records from the boroughs and courts.

The most complete record of tithe maps since Domesday is at the Bodleian Library, Oxford, together with probate records (give advance notice of inquiry).

INDEX TO ILLUSTRATIONS

INDEX: PLACES

xliv

xlv

xlvii

INDEX: PEOPLE

xlix

li

lii

liii

KEY TO CAPTION CREDITS
RS : Ray South
AP : Angela Perkins
JD, SD : Judy and Stuart
Dewey
BRO : Berkshire Record Office

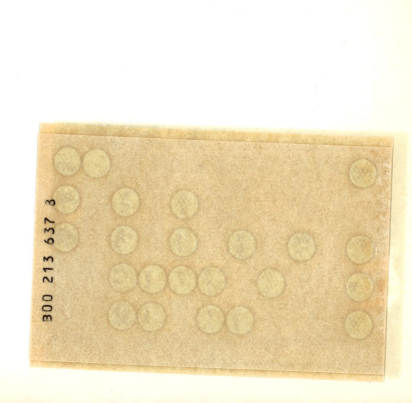

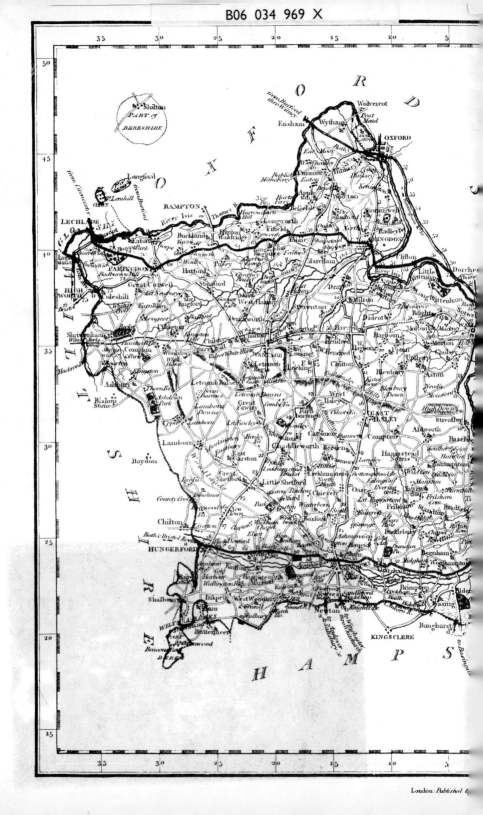

London: Published b